Refuge Ranch:

A Story for His Glory

By: Bonnie Walker

IN HIS STEPS PUBLISHING
387 N. Hall Street
Lyons, Georgia 30436 (USA)
1-912-526-6295
© 2008 by Bonnie Walker
All Rights Reserved!
First Edition: 2008
Printed in the United States of America

Bonnie Walker

The paper used in this publication meets the minimum requirements of
American National Standard for Information Sciences—Permanence of
Paper for Printed Library Materials.

Library of Congress Cataloging-in-Publication Data

Walker, Bonnie
    REFUGE RANCH: A Story for His Glory
    Bonnie Walker
    ISBN: 1-58535-180-6

*Photographs on back cover, introduction page, and last page by
Smith's Studio of Photography, Inc., Eastman, Georgia*

Refuge Ranch:

A Story for His Glory

By: Bonnie Walker

"I can do all things through Christ
who strengthens me."
(Phillippians 4:13)

Dedicated to:

My dear, sweet Heavenly Father.

Some people think that without the children this story would not be possible, but I know that without You there would be no story! I praise You for the wonderful, precious relationship that we share —
Abba, I love You!

Your Daughter,

Bonnie

Contents

*F*oreword

Every child deserves a place to belong with someone to love them. I believe that is the heart of God. Family is where we are supposed to experience God's love, be nurtured, taught, challenged and prepared for life. If our families are broken or non-existent, then we are broken too . . . and the cycle begins. There are millions of children in the world trapped in the cycle of abandonment and rejection. Lost and alone!

Jesus came to seek and to save that which was lost. Once He takes us into His forever family, He sends us out to find others. Bonnie and Billy Walker take that commission very seriously. This family of 21 children is a walking testimony to the Father heart of God. I have personally witnessed their amazing, abundant, unconditional love for each other. They are living their lives with holy abandon, and investing themselves in the things that matter to God. In God's economy there is always room for one more. Just ask Bonnie and Billy Walker—they know firsthand!

I pray that as you read this book you will be challenged to wholeheartedly jump into the deep plans God has for your life. It will be an adventure beyond anything you could imagine.

Terry Meeuwsen—Co-host, The 700 Club

Introduction

Dear Readers,

Much prayer and thoughtful consideration has gone into discerning how the Lord would have His story here at Refuge Ranch told. What style and format would be best suited to glorify Him?

Through what I believe to be the Lord's leading, I have chosen the one of which I am most familiar and most comfortable. It is the same format that I use daily in journaling my time with Father. Now some have cautioned me that this method is far too personal. It makes them feel uncomfortable as if they are ease-dropping in my private prayer closet. For those of you with such tendencies, let me put your mind at ease. It is Father who has told me that I am no longer to be a closed garden (Song of Solomon 4:12), but that I am to allow His Holy Spirit wind to "Blow upon my garden, that its spices (healing fragrances) may flow out" (Song of Solomon 4:16) and be a blessing to others.

This book is more than just a story about a family crazy enough to adopt 18 children. It is a pilgrimage of one's life, my life, my spiritual journey. But more is involved than just my life. Our children's lives have also been put on public display. Therefore, to shield them from any unnecessary pain and to help prevent any feelings of exploitation, I will not give full and gory details of each one's abuse and neglect. I will seek to share enough information of the things they have suffered so that you have some idea of "from whence they have come," so that you may be able to join with us as we praise our God for His restoration and healing. We do not focus on the negatives, nor do we want you to focus on those things. But neither do we want to give a false impression of being the perfect family. We're not! We are just a family who loves the Lord. We believe that the negative things in life get far too much attention, so we choose to focus on the positive aspects like God's love, healing, and restoration. We have been accused of living in a "bubble" instead of in the real world, which, praise God, is probably true to a large extent. We have strived to hone our lives down to one goal and one purpose—to glorify the LORD, Jesus Christ! His glory is our heart's motive for this story being told.

So grab yourself a cup of coffee or hot cocoa. Pull up a chair and relax. I eagerly invite you to share in this, my journey. Please, be at ease. You are welcome here.

My prayer is that you will be blessed and drawn closer to Father by having accompanied me on my spiritual pilgrimage here at Refuge Ranch. My desire is that this not be just another book to read, but an experience that will draw you like a magnet into a closer more intimate relationship with Father!

Love and Prayers,
Bonnie Walker

Prelude

December 10, 1974
Is It Real?

I took a walk the other day, just walking along for fun. I happened upon this pond. I had been there before -- in my dreams, with someone holding my hand. The pond was just as beautiful as it had been in my dream. The trees were showing off their new spring leaves, while wildflowers bloomed profusely in every direction my eyes traveled. The grass at the edge of the pond was lush and green. The wind was blowing gently, just enough to rustle my hair. The frogs were talking to me, and the birds were singing for me. I was beginning to feel that maybe I was mistaken, that I hadn't been there before. Then she came, a graceful heron. She flew in at the far end of the pond and landed in a clump of bushes. The feeling was back. I knew that bird! Some mysterious force made me begin to walk towards the heron. I walked around the pond to the far end. The heron flew away, and there in the bushes was a nest with her young in it. Then I remembered. "He" had been there with me in my dream. He had held my hand. He had seen the heron fly in, and had gone with me to see the nest. I remember!

We were in love! The sun rose and shone around him. I remember peering into the nest with him looking over my shoulder and squeezing my hand as he said, "We'll raise a family like that one day, and love them as much as we love each other. . ."

"Bonnie! Wake up! You'll be late for school."
"But Mama, I've been . . . dreaming?"

Dreaming? Yes, but who would have ever believed that it would be a dream to come true? That I was not the only one dreaming, but that God had placed the same dream within a young man's heart less than ten miles away. Greater still is the fact that the dream originated in Father's heart before we both were even born. Now, how wonderfully wild is that? So, to the Creator of all dreams worth dreaming --- here is my story.

Chapter One

The Beginning . . .
Muddling Through . . .
Is That You?

Well, Dear Father,

It's me again, Your little girl. I need Your help. You said to tell my story. Well actually, it is Your story, and I hardly know where to begin. Where did this story start? One of the first things that comes to mind is pain! How many times do You use pain to get us to look to You? The pain was almost more than I could bear, or at least so I thought at the time. My heart cried out over and over, "Why? I don't understand! Why? Why? Why?"

It was February 1985. A friend had came over to share her good news. She was expecting, with child, in the family way. I smiled. I congratulated her. I said all the right and proper things that you are supposed to say. But inside -- I was crying. My heart felt as if it were shattered. I had lost my baby just a few weeks earlier, but I had not told a soul. Just You and Billy were all that knew. I was so confused, so hurt. Katrina had just turned one, but I was almost overcome with a burden, a burning passion, a deep desperation for more children that did not make sense, even to me.

But I'm getting ahead of myself. Who would have thought on October 22, 1975 just how enormous Your plans actually were? There we were, standing before the pastor in my parents' home, pledging our love to each other, both barely more than children ourselves. Not understanding the magnitude of what we were saying, much less the magnitude of Your plans, Father. In May of that year I celebrated my seventeenth birthday. Billy, bless his heart, was still "wet behind the ears" (as we say on the farm) from having just turned seventeen the month prior to the wedding. Lord, looking back, I realize we stirred up quite a stew. Here I was a straight A student, on first-string girls' Varsity basketball team, and a high school drop out to boot. Billy on the other didn't apply himself to schooling much. Not that He wasn't smart enough to do so. Being the practical kind of guy that he was, he just did not see the point of packing his head with what seemed to him to be useless information. He could calculate hog prices with feed and corn ratios in his head faster than most people can do on a calculator. What more did he need? Oh yeah, besides a wife and family. So that's where I came in. We had dated for a year. Deciding to marry on the anniversary of our first date which had been October 22, 1974.

One day, as we worked to fix up an old house on Billy's parents' farm, I remember asking him, if he could choose, would he rather me be at home with him each day or go to school. He said he had rather me be with him, but for me to do what I wanted. Well Lord, You know that was all it took. Our plans had been for him to quit school and work with his daddy on the farm, while I would finish my last year of school.

In the spring, I had already notified my coach that there would be no basketball playing for me my senior year. Remember what he said, Lord, when I told him my heart just was not in it? His reply was if my heart was not in it, then there was no point in me playing. A wise man, that coach! I had chased a basketball since I was in sixth grade, but now my heart was chasing a dream. I wonder if my coach saw even then how much of an all or nothing person I am. But anyways, with Billy voicing his desire to have me near all day, my course was set.

Billy and Bonnie's Wedding
October 22, 1975

There would be no schooling, no graduation, and I couldn't have been more happy. We were so in love that I was totally enveloped in my own little world -- one shear bubble of joy! I am sad to say that it never one time crossed my self-ish thought patterns as to how this decision would affect my parents, nor the snickers and innuendoes that my brother would have to face because of my actions. I was too wrapped up in me, or Billy I should say, to care that my selfishness was causing others pain.

To this day I am astounded at my parents' restraint. Lord, I do not even remember them being angry about it. I recall one time that they sat me down face to face and asked, "Are you sure this is what you want to do?" I replied, "I'm positive." They never said another word. But it hurt them, I am sure, and for that I am sorry. But at the time I was madly, hopelessly, romantically in love. The sun rose and set in Billy Walker. He was everything I had ever wanted in my husband -- a Christian, a hard worker, easy-going, even tempered, and he wanted lots of children also. Plus, he was dark-haired and handsome! What more could a girl ask for! So we said our "I do"s and "I will"s, and set off on our honeymoon. We decided to cut it short so that we could come home to start our lives together in our newly repainted little house. At least the inside was newly painted. The outside was a very weathered looking white -- more weathered than white. It wasn't much to look at, but to us it was heavenly. We didn't mind that there was no running water. The outhouse was out the back door and over the fence. There were cracks in the floor that you could see the chickens walking under the house. No heat, except the old wood fireplace and the heat of our young love to keep us warm. You know, Lord, I can't even remember how many weeks before they actually got the well dug and running water in the house. We finally made a crude shower on the back of the house, just a shower head with a four by four metal ten enclosure with a cloth flap over the entrance. Remembering it makes me laugh. It is amazing what you will do and do without when you are young and in love. How You must have been chuckling at us also. Two little kids playing house! What fun! What innocence!

Our First Home

Later that fall, Billy's pony had a foal which Billy gave to me. I actually had a horse of my very own. I was euphoric. Father, You know how much I love horses. That Christmas I told Billy's mother that I had everything I had ever wanted except a baby. Billy was wonderful, my life was wonderful, but I was ready to start our family.

Billy, on the other hand, never jumped into anything in a hurry. But by April, either I had worn him out asking or else You had a talk with him out on that tractor. He came in from plowing, walked in the back door and announced, "I want to have a baby." When I caught my breath, I squeaked out, "Now? Right now?" He said yes, and I laughingly fell into his embrace.

Ten months later, on February 6, 1977, after a very normal, uneventful pregnancy, at 5:55 p.m., we were blessed and delighted with the arrival of our precious 6 lb. 15 oz. bundle -- Christy Marie Walker.

How thrilled we were! She had gorgeous red hair, and a

lovely complexion that would not freckle like mine. Lord, I have repented, but You remember how I hated my freckles. Never realizing as a child and young adult that even with that, You had a plan. I now have children every color of my skin from the whitest to the most brown and every shade in between. The kids have lots of fun finding the freckle or patch of white on my arms that exactly matches the color of their individual skin tone. Looking back, Your sovereign hand was certainly at work.

Christy was a happy, obedient child. She began talking at an extremely early age, and as of today at lunch, she has not stopped. My one regret is that I was not content with each age she was at any given time. I really had no idea of the magnitude of the marvelous gift that You had entrusted into our care. I was constantly wishing she could talk, or walk, or reach whatever the next developmental stage she was approaching. Father, You have worked quite a miracle with my lack of patience, haven't You? Thank You for that.

Christy Marie in Her
1st Frilly Dress

There were other areas, besides impatience, that needed just as much if not more straightening out. But You have been faithful and extremely longsuffering.

During the last month of my pregnancy with Christy, we began to build our new home, which probably was not the best timing in the world, considering I had a new baby to care for. But when you are young, you can be foolish and get away with it, or so it seems. I had grown up poor, and the possibility had never entered my mind that I would one day get to build a brand new home. Father, You lovingly watched as I went overboard as I was so prone to do. For quite some time I allowed this house to be an idol. I was obsessed with keeping it looking like it did the first day we moved in when Christy was barely four months old. It amazes me how longsuffering You are with Your foolish children like me.

You would think new baby, new house -- a perfect time to be content. But something was missing. We had jokingly told everyone before we married that we were going to have ten children. Everyone's comment was, "Wait until they have one." Well, we had one, and we still wanted ten. Secretly, I believed that You had told me more than that, but everyone had laughed and ridiculed us so about wanting ten children that there was no way that I was going to share that little piece of information with anyone.

So with an aching hunger for more children that I could not explain, we planned another pregnancy. Christy was just two months shy of her second birthday when we decided to have another baby. We had planned it meticulously so that the baby would be born as close to Billy's birthday in September as humanly possible. I was so excited -- the baby's due date was one week after Billy's birthday, his birthday present from me. But it was not to be. After barely announcing the pregnancy on New Year's night of 1979, I took the flu. After a week of raging fever, I lost our little baby. I was devastated! I understood that the fever had damaged the fetus. I understood that, yes, I was young and could have other children. But I didn't want other children, I wanted my baby. The "why's" sent me spiraling into a sea of depression. The only blessing that I could see was that at least I had Christy at home to hold and cuddle, but that didn't stop the pain. In Your mercy, You touched the heart of a dear lady who had suffered far worse than I had to come and share her story. She had carried her little daughter full term. Her baby had suffered brain damage due to a difficult delivery in which forceps were misused. This caused the death of her little baby girl. For the first time in weeks, I could really *see* that it could have been worse. Others had said so, but they were not walking in my pain, and I could not believe them. You used this woman to reach my heart that had become extremely cold.

I am older and wiser now, but at the tender age of twenty I thought life stopped with every tragedy. Lord, did I ever have a lot to learn.

Time passed, and we rolled into spring. The flowers were blooming, baby animals were being born and hatched. You, in Your wondrous way, opened my womb once again. Our second child was on the way! But this pregnancy was far different from the first with Christy.

Three months into the pregnancy, I was in a lot of pain. And Father, I was terrified! I lived in constant fear of miscarrying. The constant pain was nerve wracking. I spent the majority of the last six months of the pregnancy on the couch, except for going to church and weekly grocery trips. Where with Christy, I had carried her so high that she hindered my breathing, I was carrying this baby so low that I felt as if it was constantly about to fall out. I feared placenta-pivia and a mirage of other dreaded things that hovered over me like a lead blanket.

By the time my due date arrived, I was an emotional mess. Lord, if only someone would have told me about spiritual warfare, so much of my anguish could have been avoided. At the time, I didn't know a demon from a doorknob, but I would soon learn. Precious Father, You were going to make sure of that!

The delivery was as difficult as the pregnancy had been. A

two day ordeal, but what a blessing You had in store for us. Josey Lois Walker finally arrived safe and sound on Saturday, January 19, 1980. She weighed 8 lbs. and 14 oz. . With blonde, curly hair and big blue eyes, she would soon be dubbed "our smiling angel." And an angel she was! I did not realize it at the time, but it took a while for me to recuperate from the emotional trauma of the entire pregnancy.

Christy (nearly 3) Showing Off
Baby Sister, Josey Lois
January 23, 1980

Billy, bless his heart, had been such a trooper through the whole thing. I'm sure it wasn't easy for him either, seeing me so upset and in so much pain, but he never complained. We thought at the time that the pain was caused by the baby being so low. It would be years later before we would discover the real culprit.

But life progressed on with us joyfully raising our two precious darlings. Christy loved doting on her little sister, and Josey adored her in return. We started teaching Christy to share and give as soon as she could understand. So, sharing with baby sister came easy for her. As the girls grew, we continually let them know that there were other little kids out in the world that didn't have the blessings that they did. I believe that training, along with Your love, is what has enabled them to open their hearts to so many siblings.

They were thrilled three years later to hear that another baby was on the way. It had taken a long time, but I had finally got desperate enough for another child that my desire over-rode my fear of another pregnancy. Billy and I both were apprehensive, but we both were determined to have more children.

Josey, "The Prairie Princess"
(4 years old)

Oh Father, how blessed we were. Easy pregnancy, easy delivery! Katrina Victoria Mae Walker arrived on January 23, 1984, two weeks before her official due date. She was a healthy, beautiful, black-haired, 8 lb. 1 oz. baby girl. Everyone teased me about having eaten so much chocolate syrup that it turned her hair black. I remember asking my mama if it was okay for me to be so tickled over another little girl. I was feeling guilty because I was so elated at our precious baby girl with the head full of raven black hair. Was it wrong to not be disappointed for Billy's sake about not having a boy? Now, the question seems foolish. Should I have been disappointed at the beautiful, perfect gift that You gave? Absolutely not! You give only good and perfect gifts. Thank You, Father, for each of our girls. What blessings! Each daughter is so precious, so alike, and yet so extremely different. One red-haired with fair to tan complexion, the second blonde, curly-haired with freckles popping out everywhere, and the last black-haired with her daddy's dark complexion. Even in our biological children, You had a plan. You knew as the years unfolded that no one would be able to draw a line and separate the adopted from the biological. You are so neat in the planning. Not even the tiniest detail passes by You.

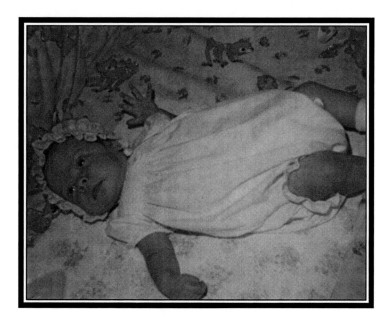

Katrina Victoria Mae Walker
(2 months old)

So here we were—a normal, all-American family of five. Everyone had said wait until we had two children, then we wouldn't want any more. Then it was just wait until that third one gets here. Our hearts were still desiring a large family. We had everything we needed to be content, but deep within there was that uneasy, aching, longing for . . . more children.

Your Searching Child,
Bonnie

Chapter Two

God Spoke...

Father,

You know that "not knowing" what a person wants to be or do when they grow up is something I have never really understood. Remember in the sixth grade when my science teacher went around the room asking each of us the all important question, "What do you want to do when you grow up?" My reply was the same thing it had been for as long as I could remember -- "I'm going to get married and have a house full of kids." To which he indignantly replied, "Oh, no you're not! You're going to be a scientist or biologist or an astronaut -- or something else worthwhile to mankind." I tried to convince him, but he wouldn't listen. He could look at it on the bright side; he was half right. Raising Christian soldiers is certainly something worthwhile to mankind. From Your point of view, I expect it is probably one of the most worthwhile contributions to society -- earthly and heavenly.

But anyway -- I have always known, not the magnitude,

not the whole picture, but enough to know that there were lots of children. I think You probably thought it was wiser to let me know upfront, so that I didn't aggravate the stew out of You (figuratively speaking, of course) by constantly bombarding You with questions. My daddy raised me to believe that the only foolish question was the question never asked. Let's just suffice it to say that not too many "foolish questions" ever stay lodged in my brain. I'm like Joel was at four years old, or, on second thought, maybe he's like me. Every time Billy lets him go to the cow sale or to work with him, Billy comes home saying that Joel asked a million and one questions.

But getting back to that memorable day in February 1985, a friend had come over and shared her good news about her pregnancy. This was not the first time that I had struggled with feelings of jealousy or unfairness. I would see a young mother in town with three or four little kids, unkempt and bedraggled. But it wasn't the physical stuff that ripped at my heart. It was the fact that that same mother would be cussing those precious babies or jerking them around, threatening them with "Just wait til . . .". My heart would scream within me, "Why God? Why? Give them to me. It's not fair; it's not fair!"

Truthfully though, even with news of others' pregnancies, my heart would hurt. Surely, Lord, I am not Your only child that has struggled to rejoice at others' good fortune. It was not that I wished harm nor barrenness on others, but it just intensified my own pain somehow. Having just suffered my second miscarriage, I was a jumble of "Why's". I didn't know, and I couldn't see. But You had a plan, and what a wonderful plan it was.

I will never forget that day. It was the first time that I actually heard Your voice. No, I take that back. That was the first time that You spoke that I recognized it as Your voice. To this day, I am not sure if it was audible or if You spoke within my spirit, but I knew it was You and I knew what You said.

Josey (6), Katrina (2) & Christy (9)

I had made all the polite responses to my friend's news. I had smiled until my face felt stiff and frozen. All the time my heart was breaking. I walked her out the door to her car. We said our good-byes. As I turned to re-enter the house, I felt a hand gently patting me comfortingly on my shoulder. Then I heard Your voice saying:

"I will make you the mother of many children!"

My spirit leapt within me. I began to rejoice, but I had no idea of the magnitude of what You had just said. Nor did I realize the path that Your plan would take. Right then, right there, I knew that You knew and that was enough -- at least for the time being.

Three years later, after You had led us into fostering and adoption, I penned the following poem that so describes how I felt that day that You said You'd make me . . .

The Mother of Many Children

The mother of many children
Is what You said I'd be;
    "I'll make you the mother of many children,"
Is how You comforted me.

My heart was near to breaking
The day You told me that;
    As you gently and lovingly reached down
And gave my shoulder a pat.

The comfort that I felt,
The peace that filled my soul,
    The joy that this brought
Can't be measured or even told.

The mother of many children,
How my soul longs to be;
    How many will be enough, Lord?
Ten? Fifteen? Possibly Twenty?

No one understands, Lord,
No one but You and me.
    Please fill up this hole, Lord,
Aching inside of me.
    I am so very grateful
For the five You've given me,
    For the three that I've borrowed,
If only temporarily.

But oh, how my heart yearns
For more feet beneath my table,
    And more hungry mouths to feed.
More children, Lord, You're able.

You know, Lord,
They call me crazy, but that's okay by me.
   I'm going to keep on being Your servant
For all the world to see.

   Dear Lord, my prayer to You now,
Is what 'er Your will may be.
   Dear Lord, help me be ready
For any possibility.

   Guide my thoughts and feet, Lord,
And do not let me step,
   Not one inch away, Lord,
From the path that You have kept.

AMEN!

But once again I am jumping the gun. There was more pain to endure first. August of 1985 -- another miscarriage! Then in October, another pregnancy. Oh, surely this time would be different. Everything seemed to be going fine, but I kept hearing one word in my spirit that I did not understand. "Surgery!"

I didn't realize that You were trying to warn me. The second week in December, just over two months into the pregnancy, the doctor could not find a heartbeat. He scheduled me for a sonogram the following morning. Foolishly, I went alone. Except I wasn't alone, was I Father? You were there with me.

After my much persistent questioning, the technician confirmed my worst fear. My baby was dead. No heartbeat. No movement at all, just a tiny, black looking pea shape. Oh God! I felt like part of me died that day. Three miscarriages in eleven months. My heart cried things that day that no one ever talks about. "Where was my God who was supposed to be protecting me?"

I remember phoning Billy before I left the hospital. I remember being in the car thinking, "Bonnie, you're too upset to drive. Just sit here until you calm down." Lord, the next thing I recall was about half way home when I started screaming! I just kept screaming, "I don't want to hear it! I don't want to hear it!" Invariably, one of the first things that is said to a mother who has miscarried is, "You're young, and you can have another baby." Oh God, how I hated those words! I didn't want to hear them again. I didn't want another baby; I wanted my baby. I was in shock and nearly hysterical, but somehow You managed to get through to me enough that I realized it wasn't safe to be driving in my emotional condition.

I started thinking if I could just get to a church. I remembered that there was one at the next town. I decided to try to make it to the little church. I did, but the door was locked. To this day, Father, I think it's the saddest thing that a church door has to be locked. Going back to the car, I just got in and sat down. Father, only You know how long I just sat there. I don't remember praying, but perhaps I did. To be truthful Lord, I don't remember anything about the rest of that day.

Later that week a DNC was done, and we were told to wait three months and try again. When January 10, 1986 arrived, I received my answer of what I had kept hearing in the fall about "surgery". That day, after a shopping trip to town with my sister-in-law, I was attacked with appendicitis. At lunch, I hadn't really felt like eating, but I didn't think much about it. But by the time we returned home, I began to realize something wasn't right. Billy came in from the cow sale that night to find me collapsed on the floor in so much pain that I was unable to get up. All I could say was get me some help. By the time he was able to get a babysitter, I had miraculously stopped hurting. I was extremely sore, and it hurt to walk, but the pain had lessened considerably.

We headed to the emergency room anyway to see what was going on. I suspected appendix, but Billy, bless his heart, was hoping it was just a severe virus. This is one time I can truthfully say that I wish he had been right.

Surgery followed the next day, within a month's time of my last miscarriage. For once, I thought I had a reason of "Why?". Being three months pregnant and having to have surgery would not have been a good thing. I could see Your hand working a little there, and it eased some of the pain.

Your Listening Little Girl,
Bonnie

Christy, 9 years old

Chapter Three

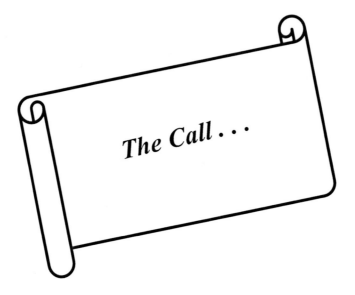

Dear Sweet Abba,

How I remember this part of the story as if it were yester-
day! It was March of 1986, and You were up to something.
Well, You are always up to something, but this was the first
time that I realized before hand that You were wanting to tell
me or show me something. At that time it wasn't common for
me to say, "God's fixing to do something. There's a 'holy
hush' in the heavenlies." A holy hush is just my term for
when I sense all of Heaven is holding their breath and thinking, "Watch this!" in anticipation of what You are about to do.
I love it, Lord! It is so exciting! But then life with You is anything but dull!

Now, where was I? Oh, yes, You were wanting to reveal
something to me. Our pastor preached that Sunday morning
on I Samuel 3:7-10 (NKJV).

"Now Samuel did not yet know the Lord, nor was the word of the Lord yet revealed to him. And the Lord called Samuel again the third time. So he arose and went to Eli, and said, 'Here I am, for you did call me.' Then Eli perceived that the Lord had called the boy. Therefore Eli said to Samuel, 'Go, lie down; and it shall be, if He calls you, that you must say, 'Speak, Lord, for Your servant hears.' So Samuel went and lay down in his place. Now the Lord came and stood and called as at other times. 'Samuel! Samuel!' and Samuel answered, 'Speak, for Your servant hears.'"

I was so moved in my spirit I could barely sit still. As the altar call was given, I hurried to the front. I told our pastor that I knew You were calling me to something just as You had called Samuel. I knew it was something to do with children, but I didn't know what. Like Samuel, I was willing to say, "Speak, for Your servant hears (is listening)!"

That week I determined to seek You more to find some answers. I shared with the young ladies group that I was teaching on Wednesday nights what was going on and asked them to please be praying for me. I needed to know what God was saying.

Saturday of that week, You sent another visitor. This woman had recently miscarried, also. We were commiserating together. She had no children, and I had three, but she wasn't in the anguish about more kids that I was in. I was telling her that what I didn't understand was that if You didn't want me to have more children then why was I so consumed with the desire to have more. Abruptly, she stated, "You need to be a foster parent!" I didn't even hesitate, but quickly exclaimed, "NO!" I told her that there was no way that I could take in kids, love them, and then let them go back into the messes they had come out of. She left shortly thereafter, but Your Spirit didn't.

I went back to my sewing. As I sewed I heard, "Be a foster parent!" I was too spiritually immature to immediately recognize it was You, Father. Truth be told, I would probably have still said, "No!", but You were persistent. Just as You kept calling Samuel over and over, You kept repeating, "Be a foster parent." I would say, "I can't." But Your reply was always the same, "Be a foster parent." You weren't angry, just lovingly firm and determined. I finally gave up trying to sew. By this time I was crying so hard that I couldn't see where to stitch the seams anyway. Father, adopting we had considered. We had even discussed it some prior to us getting married, but fostering? That was "a horse of a different color", as the saying goes. The only thing that had ever been mentioned about it was -- "No way!" But like You say in Isaiah 55:8,

"For My thoughts are not your thoughts, neither are your ways my ways, saith the Lord."

I just didn't realize at the time the magnitude of truth in that word. I left the sewing machine blinded by tears with what sounded like a stuck record playing over and over in my head. "Be a foster parent. Be a foster parent." I remember falling to my knees, wailing to You, "I can't! I can't!" For by this time, even I had sense enough to know who was speaking. Finally, after what seemed like an eternity, I collapsed across my recliner, begrudgingly surrendering, but surrendering nevertheless. It's by Your grace that You didn't strike me dead after my belligerent remark. I can't believe now how I tossed this comment at You. "Okay, but You have got to give me something." I reached for my Bible, opened it up, and a scripture seemed to literally magnify and fly off the page into my face, almost striking me physically. It was so forceful. Repeatedly, I'd cried out to You, "I can't. I can't." Your rebuttal was,

"I can do all things through Christ, who strengthens me." (Philippians 4:13).

With that word, peace came. It is amazing how You meet us right where we are. I would be in trouble big time now if I argued with You like that. Now, it would be rebellion. Then, I was reacting immaturely out of my fear. Thank You, Lord, for grace and growth! You could see the big picture. You knew that we would need all the training and preparation for the years ahead.

But first I had to share with Billy what You had said. We had a long talk and both agreed to pray about it for a couple of weeks. At the end of that time, we were in full agreement. Yes, this was God, and we would obey.

What happened next was pure manipulation on my part. I had to learn the hard way that You can not be manipulated. I figured that since we had agreed to obey You that You would not mind letting us have one more baby before we got started on Your plans. I was wrong. I got pregnant, and miscarried once again. Four miscarriages in sixteen months. I had had enough. It was time to get on with Your plans. We contacted the Department of Family and Children Services to begin the tedious process of getting approved by the state to become foster parents.

One year later, in May of 1987, the phone call that we'd been waiting for finally came. We were trained. We were ready. And we had so-o-o-o much to learn! Our first foster son was on the way. A five year old little boy that needed a place to stay for a few months. I was ecstatic. My joy soon turned to weeping.

I will never forget his first bath and the black water that I rinsed out of his blonde hair. As I washed his hair, fighting back my tears, I wondered how anyone could let a child remain so filthy. You really grabbed a hold of my heart in a big way, didn't You, Father?

The sweet little fellow left after a few months, and I survived. At least we still had our three girls, and they were a comfort beyond words. Shortly after this little fellow left, we decided it was time to take care of a problem that was steadily worsening. The pain that had started during my second pregnancy was gradually consuming my life.

Doctor after doctor was stumped. There was nothing left to

do but surgery. In hopes of getting relief from the constant pain, I readily agreed to the surgery to remove my uterus and one ovary. The doctor was hopeful of being able to save the other ovary, which he did, at least for the time being. I will never forget the day after surgery when the doctor walked in and put a name to the pain that had plagued me for years -- Taylor's syndrome! He explained that it's a very rare condition of varicose veins in the pelvic area. In my case, enormous varicose veins encased my uterus and one ovary. It was an absolute miracle that I had been able to carry and deliver Josey or Katrina. If one of those large bulging veins had of ruptured and began hemorrhaging during the pregnancy, my life, as well as the baby's, would have been at risk. Thank You, Father, for Your grace and mercy. You had been there all along keeping me safe, and I wasn't crazy after all. It is so unnerving going, going, going to doctors, and no one can put a name to what is wrong. People begin to raise their eyebrows, and you can just hear their thought processes. "This woman is just a hypochondriac." But finally there was a name to what was wrong with me, and I had my answer as to why I couldn't carry any more babies.

The relief of having an answer was bitter-sweet because now we knew for certain that there would be no more biological children. With every loss, there is some grieving, but here again You were right there to meet my every need. And what a miracle -- I was no longer continually suffering physical pain. Thank You!

Your grateful daughter,
Bonnie

Chapter Four

Following The Call...

Well Father,

I've heard it said that when You close one door, You open another. I've found this to be so true. I recovered nicely from surgery. A few months later in October another call came.

Our caseworker wanted to know would we consider fostering two little girls, ages 7 and 10. Their mother had abandoned the family when the children were very young. The girls had been in and out of children's homes and passed from "pillar to post" with various relatives. The youngest had been in seventeen different homes during her short seven years. To compound matters, they had suffered all kinds of abuse. The aging father could no longer care for them and had gone to the Department of Family and Children Services for help. Full of idealisms and over-confidence in my own abilities, I joyfully and eagerly anticipated their coming.

So in late October of 1987, Peggy (10) and Cindy (7) arrived. I had been so excited that I was unable to sleep, dancing around the house and bouncing off the walls. How my heart swelled with love when I saw them. The caseworker had hinted that these two might possibly come up for adoption. I felt instinctively that they were ours. Upon studying birth dates, we were amazed to discover that Peggy and Christy had shared the same hospital nursery as infants. Now, ten years later, here they were sharing the same bedroom. Lord, You are breathtakingly amazing with Your intricate workings in our lives.

Cindy Lachelle - 8 years old

Everything was wonderful, blissfully so . . . for two weeks. Then the honeymoon was over, and the testing began. My first inkling that we were in for rough waters was when Peggy picked up the piano stool in a fit of rage and flung it across the living room floor. Cindy immediately began to follow suit with one temper tantrum after another. For months, we tried to hide the disaster that was taking place in our home. Finally, Billy said we had to tell the department. Their solution— move and separate the girls. We flatly, firmly, refused even the thought, much less the suggestion. God had given these girls to us. We had to find some way to help them.

Peggy Rae - 11 years old

Peggy was all tomboy. She loved outdoors. She was such a help doing any and everything in the yards. Even though she'd been severely burned as a toddler, requiring several surgeries, she was a beautiful child. Her compassion for those less fortunate was a wonder to behold. Her fingers seemed to fly over the piano keyboard with an instinctive ear for music.

Cindy, on the other hand, loved kittens and baby dolls. Dressing up and wearing mama's makeup were her favorite pastime activities. And sing -- she had the voice of an angel. With her beautiful smile and dimples flashing, she was quite the little charmer.

Give up our girls? No way! We began a desperate search to find the help they needed. We asked foster parenting classes everywhere we went the same question. What do we do? We tried counseling. Nothing worked consistently. Things would seem to improve; then the situation would plummet.

Even in the midst of all this, we proceeded with adoption

proceedings, much to the trepidation of the few family members and friends that we had confided in about our situation. On September 20, 1989, Peggy Rae (named after her Daddy) and Cindy Lachelle became legal members of the Walker household. Father, we were so hopeful that the stability of a permanent family would bring peace to their souls. Such was not the case. It is only by Your grace that we survived the next seven years.

What I would have given to have known then what I know now! I finally did what I should have done at the start. I cried out to You to show us how to help these two precious children who had suffered so much abuse at the hands of the enemy. You've taught me so much about spiritual warfare, inner healing, and how to minister that healing to others. Now I'm much better equipped to meet the needs of troubled children. But alas, we did the best we could with what little knowledge we had. It's comforting that You have given me absolute assurance that our Peggy Rae and Cindy Lachelle will both be healed and restored in Jesus' name. Father, I praise You for that in advance. They are our first two adopted daughters, and we praise You for them.

Before Peggy and Cindy's adoption in September, February of 1989 brought another blessing. Greyson Tyler arrived in our home. He came on February 6th which was Christy's twelfth birthday. She immediately dubbed him as "her birthday present."

A couple of weeks prior to this a caseworker from another county mentioned that they had a little Hispanic baby boy that would need a home. He was in the hospital in traction with a broken leg. Father, I know You remember, after the foster parent meeting, how I danced around Billy as we went down the sidewalk. I kept saying over and over, "A baby boy, Billy! Just think, a baby boy!" He thought I had gone nuts! He still does, bless his heart!

It was nearly two weeks before we were officially notified. It was two weeks of little sleep and extreme impatience on my part. I set the crib up in our room. With five little girls and only three bedrooms, we didn't have a lot of options as far as space goes, but I could hardly wait for his arrival.

Easter Elegance
Greyson (4 months), Peggy (12), Josey (9), Katrina (5)
Cindy (9) & Christy (12)

The Department had told us that he'd suffered multiple fractures all at varying degrees of healing. Two of these consisted of hairline skull fractures. Father, thank You for protecting him. The only lasting problems those caused are neurological damage to his motor skills. In layman's terms that just means he's clumsy and not very coordinated. The doctor said Greyson would never make a great athlete. Hey, we can live with that. As for the broken leg, well, smart, intelligent person that I am -- I braced myself for the worst. I don't know what Billy was expecting, but me? Father, I imagined what I believed was a worse case scenario. The baby would arrive with his leg in a cast from hip to foot. Not! To my shock and horror, two and a half month old Greyson arrived in a body cast from his chest down. I was speechless. When the sheriff's car pulled up with the worker in the front seat holding Greyson laid across her lap, I nearly cried. This was nothing like I had envisioned or imagined. I remember thinking, "Oh God!"

It took weeks to figure out how to cuddle him with that cumbersome cast, plus weeks before I could lay him on his back without him screaming. Changing diapers was painstakingly tedious. Soiled ones usually took as long as thirty minutes and sometimes longer than that. The cast had to be lined with Saran wrap, and then the opening was packed with cotton gauze. I was so excited when the day came to have the cast removed. After weeks of nursing and meticulously cleaning, I'd finally get to cuddle my baby and give him an all over bath. I don't know what I was expecting his little body to look like, but what I saw wasn't what I had anticipated. His little leg flopped completely sideways with no muscle tone, and his skin was dark brown and flaky like a snake's skin. He looked pitiful. The doctor was more than pleased. He praised me for taking such excellent care of Greyson. He said most babies and children like that have open sores when a cast is removed. Father, he might have thought it was wonderful, but it broke my heart.

As if all this wasn't enough to handle, Greyson has a brown complexion. What color is prejudice? I'm not sure, but I know that it is very ugly. The first day our dear worker, who was older and wiser than us, knew we were about to hit some prejudiced tidal waves. She calmly and quietly asked, "Is he too dark?" Father, I was still in shock. Holding this precious gift from You in my lap. I looked at her with tears in my eyes and asked her a question. "If we don't tend to him, who is?" I'll never forget what Billy said, "I don't care if he's *green*, he's not going anywhere!" Oh Father, Father, thank You for such a man who looks with eyes of love, just like You do. If everyone had Billy's heart of love, there would be no homeless or orphaned children.

The other thing that tormented us for the next three and a half years was the emotional roller coaster ride of, "He's going back to his birth parents." "No, he's staying with you all."

"No, he's going back." "No, he's staying." This was absolute torture to us emotionally. But here again, Your grace sustained us.

The years passed quickly with Greyson growing by leaps and bounds. He was adored by his five doting, big sisters, not to mention Billy and myself, which probably accounted for him always being the center of attention. What a blessing! Our first little boy! Greyson loved dressing up like a cowboy, going to work with his daddy, and "reading" encyclopedias. Finally, the long, awaited and hoped for day arrived. On August 31, 1992, we received his adoption papers! Hallelujah! So, with three biological and three adopted children, our family was slowly taking shape.

Cindy, Breathtakingly Beautiful!
(11 years old)

Father, it was during these years, from 1987 to May of 1993, that You sent ten foster children, each with his or her individual set of needs and problems, but You were continually teaching and training us. The biggest need by far of each child was the need to know that someone loved them, that You loved them, Father. This "temporary" parenting was extremely hard on us emotionally, but we praise You for Your sufficient grace. We are so grateful that You allowed us the privilege to adopt three of these children as our very own.

Peggy, Blissfully Peaceful
(15 years old)

As our family increased, so did our needs. Another sign of Your hand of blessing was Your provision for the new addition to the house. In 1989, You increased our 1,800 square

foot three bedroom home to 2,400 square feet with five bedrooms. Thank You! We had begun to feel somewhat cramped.
If we could have glimpsed into the future, we didn't know the
meaning of the word cramped.

Your Learning Daughter,
Bonnie

Chapter Five

Tug of War . . .
God's Way?
My Way?

Dear Father,

Through all this time, there was a war going on of which I was not even aware. Looking back, I see it so clearly. I was constantly running ahead of You. I was hearing what You would say, leaning to my own understanding, and not always allowing You to direct my paths, which is just opposite of Your word and ways laid out in Proverbs 3:5-6.

Time after time, I was rushing here and there, doing all the right things with all the wrong motives. How patient You have been. So much of what I did looked really good to man, but You could see my heart and knew that my exploits were done in the arm of the flesh (Jeremiah 17:5). There was a constant battle of Your way or my way. Your little girl had some "dying" to do.

It was time for my journey into the wilderness that all of Your children must take sooner or later. For years I had been crying out for You to change me into the image of Your Son,

Jesus. It was June 1991, and a major part of my transformation was about to take place. Because of spirits of rejection in my life, I had erected an idol of 'accomplishing' which won me the praise of man. I was addicted to rat racing! 'Hurry up and rush, rush' was a way of life for me. You knew that physically I couldn't hold out forever doing that, but I believe You were more concerned about where I was at spiritually. I couldn't "be still and know" You (Psalm 46:10) if I was constantly trying to accomplish one more project. I was so into striving to do and be and so needy for man's approval that I constantly worked at trying to out-do my last achievement. It was a pitiful, miserable way to live.

You told me once that You always send Your word before You send Your judgment. Well, so it was with me. Three times You warned me. You had a friend call me to issue the first warning. I needed to slow down, so that I could spend more time with You. Next, You placed a magazine article in my hands about that very thing. Then thirdly, You spoke to me in a dream.

In the dream, I was riding a four wheeler down a dirt road speeding along full throttle. I came upon this pond, and I so longed to stop and rest. It was so peaceful that I yearned to relax by the waters awhile. But alas, I couldn't. I was too busy. So I gave the pond one last longing look and sped on by. In the dream I next encountered a rattlesnake curled up in the road. I knew the snake represented the devil. In my cockiness and pride I thought, "You can't get me!" I propped my feet up high on the four wheeler so that the snake couldn't reach me. I laughed gleefully as I swerved around him continuing on my journey full speed ahead. Then the road became a dirt ramp that led right up to the edge of a cliff. I never even let up on the gas, and as I sailed off into midair I heard these words, "You're going to crash!"

I woke up with a start, remembering the dream vividly and having an instant interpretation of every aspect of it. Yes, this was definitely a warning from You, the third of three in fact!

Why I didn't listen to You will always remain a mystery to

me. I'm not sure whether to chalk it up to stupidity or stubbornness or both. But You'd sent Your warnings -- now comes the judgment.

Three years earlier, the ovary that the doctor had left when the surgery was done had been damaged some with the Taylor's Syndrome. The doctor had hoped, with the absence of a menstrual cycle, that it might not give me any more problems. Such was not the case. It, too, had gradually become more and more painful. It was surgery time again.

Greyson (3 years old)
Enjoying his homemade tractor bed!

August of 1991, I entered the hospital for what was to be routine surgery, but it turned out to be anything but routine. The surgery was Friday morning. On Saturday morning, as I was waking up, I felt like You had told me in a dream that I would have to be opened back up -- something was wrong. Lord, when I told Billy he thought I was just worrying needlessly. Even though I realized with pain medication that the dream might have been drug induced, I couldn't shake the feeling that something was very, very wrong.

By Sunday everyone else knew it, too. My abdomen was constantly swelling. I looked about eight months pregnant. I was given test after test. I was given bag after bag of antibiotics and put on constant pain medication. By late Sunday evening, a naso-gastric tube was placed through my nose and into my stomach. This was attached to a pump in hopes of emptying gases or whatever was causing the bloating. It didn't help. I was in more pain and in far worse shape than I was when I had come to the hospital. Something had to be done.

The second surgery was scheduled for Tuesday morning. So back under the knife I went. Father, I can't remember how much fluid they said they drained from my abdominal cavity, but the nurses were shocked by the quantity. They had never seen anything like it before. Lord, I remember waking up from the anesthetic and thinking, "Now I know what a meatball feels like with noodles wrapped all around it." I had wires and tubes, gadgets and gizmos going every which way, but the pain was eased. I was sore from the surgery. I felt like I'd been hit by a Mac truck, but that unbearable pain, that would start in the small of my back and consume my body, was no more . . . at least for the time being.

Finally, things were looking up. Wednesday, I made improvement. Thursday, they began to talk about letting me go home but first things first. Let's get rid of some tubes. That afternoon, the doctor removed my drain tube and super pubic catheter. Within a few hours, I knew that I was in trouble. The pressure was starting to build up in my lower back again. I tried so hard, Father, to ignore it, to pretend like it wasn't there. My nerves were shot. Physically and emotionally, I was spent. My grit was completely gone. At about 2:00 a.m., I called Billy who was at home with the kids. Weeping, I told him that I knew I wasn't coming home on Friday because the pain was returning. My abdomen had also begun to swell again. I only remember bits and pieces of the rest of the night. Father, I do remember asking the nurse for something to knock me out because I couldn't stand the pain any more. She told me that they had given me enough pain medication to kill an elephant, and that they couldn't give me any more. By the time Billy got to the hospital, my world had become a blackened tunnel with only a small circle of vision. My calm, laid back hubby raked the doctor over the coals pretty good that morning, but at least it got results. The super pubic catheter was replaced, draining another enormous amount of fluid from my abdomen. Once again the draining brought immediate relief from the pain.

Other doctors were called in to consult on my case. The urologist that was called in took one look at the tubes coming from my two catheters and said that the super pubic one wasn't even draining from my bladder. It was draining fluid from my abdominal cavity. We had to find out where the fluid was coming from.

Surgery was scheduled for the next day. My third surgery in nine days! The doctor cystoscoped me, placing a stint in my left ureter (the tube from my kidney to my bladder). It had been punctured during the first surgery and had been steadily draining urine into my abdominal cavity ever since. The stint would prevent leakage until the ureter could have time to heal.

Oh Father, what a hard lesson to learn. It took six months before I was anywhere close to regaining my strength, but one thing is for sure and certain: just as Jacob limped after his encounter with You at Peniel (Genesis 32: 24-32), I, too, continue to limp. I would rather limp in utter dependence on You, than limp spiritually if I don't take time to be with You. I learned that when You say to be still and know You, that's exactly what You mean. Father, I pray I limp the rest of my natural life, recognizing my need for You in all things that I do. I may be a slow learner when it comes to some things, but I thank You that I'm no dummy. Once I get a revelation I hang on to it, and Your little girl learned a valuable lesson. It's better to do it Father's way; the tug of war was over. Now You were free to go forward in a mighty way.

Your Humbled Little Girl,
Bonnie

Chapter Six

Adoption Days
Ahead . . .
God's Way (But He
Still Needs My Help!)

Well Father,

It was April 15, 1992, and the winds of change were blowing. I awoke that morning startled. You had just spoken to me in a dream, and my heart was still racing with the news. "Five? Did I hear You right? Did You say five?" We were to adopt a Hispanic sibling group of five! That morning, during our family Bible time, I teasingly grabbed Christy's arm, who was fifteen at the time, and said, "Quick, tell me somewhere we can run hide from God." Then I laughed and told her I was only joking. But my flesh was in somewhat of a panic. It was not that I didn't want the kids. We only had six, and we certainly wanted more, but five at one time? We had cared for enough foster kids coming into our home that I knew how hard it was. You have to help them learn where everything is from toothpaste to where their socks go. It is a major undertaking with one child. We had even tackled it with two, but five? Even "Miss I can climb any mountain" knew that this was a job for Super God! We began to prepare spiritually, emotionally, and physically. I shared with Billy and the children what You had said. We beefed up our teaching and training during our family Bible times. We were planting more and more seeds of Your word about doing, sharing, and giving unto the least of these (Matthew 25:40). We asked Your Spirit to prepare our children's hearts to share their home and parents with brothers and sisters whom they had never met.

Weeks rolled by; summer was upon us. There was no news of our new children. About this time I got this wonderful idea. I was doing things Your way, but I decided that You needed my help. That thought triggered a series of events that led to a very miserable and frustrating summer. You tell us not to lean on our own understanding with Proverbs 3:5-6, but sometimes I can be a very disobedient daughter. I reasoned that Texas was where the Hispanic children were, so I commenced to call every state agency from central to south Texas. I was impatient, not willing to wait on You. While Billy, bless his heart, just kept calmly telling me that You would send them when You were ready. Father, You and my hubby sound remarkably alike at times. Only You know the money I wasted that summer on long distance phone calls to Texas. By the end of summer, with my frantic attempts proving futile, I became very discouraged. With the kids back in school, I set my sights on other tasks, but I never lost the "knowing" of what You had said. Father, I was so immature I had yet to learn that Your every word is not immediate. I treated everything in life like a drive-in fast food restaurant. I'll place my order now, and I expect to pick it up in the next five minutes, please. I had not yet learned the art and wisdom of waiting upon the Lord (Isaiah 40:31). But I was learning -- slowly but surely.

By the spring of 1993, I was wondering what was going on? Did I really hear You? Then a phone call came from our county's Department of Family and Children's Services. Three children needed temporary care with the emphasis on temporary. Their mother was in drug rehabilitation. We were looking at a maximum of six weeks care. The children were ages three, five, and nine. We agreed to the placement, taking care of the usual rearranging and juggling required in opening our home to needy children. We were excited to be a blessing once more, but I'm not sure we would have been so eager if we could have seen two months into the future.

After a couple of weeks, we began to realize we were in for turbulent waters. The nine year old girl was very bright. It didn't take her long to figure out what she wanted, and she wanted us as her family! Father, I was not prepared for her death grip upon my heart. I had sent small children back to their birth families, and Your grace had carried me in such a way that I barely grieved. This time was different. This precious child needed a mama and knew it. Oh God, how she cried! Before they were returned to their birth mom, I did everything I could to convince her that her life with her birth mom would be better. I tried to encourage her that her mama was getting help, but the child wasn't buying any of it. Lord, You remember how the state agency even accused us of undermining her affections for her birth mom. Nothing could have been further from the truth! The last ten days prior to their departure were the worst. She cried and cried. When she wasn't crying, she was weepy and clingy. All she wanted to do was sit in my lap and cry. Father, I felt like I was dying inside, so helpless to help! I was so frustrated with the system that is supposed to be protecting children. I strongly suspected that this little girl had suffered more than just neglect. She had all the symptoms of sexual abuse, but that wouldn't be confirmed until two years later. Oh Father, it still hurts my heart. So much hurt and pain bottled up inside of one little life, and I was powerless to fix it!

As their reunification date with the birth mom drew closer, the grieving became increasingly worse. The nine year old's distress began to take its toll on the younger children as well. The five year old started with the crying spells, but at least her mind was more easily diverted than her older sister's mind. It became so bad that on departure day the agency requested that

I bring the children to their office instead of the workers coming to pick the children up. The case workers were fearful that they wouldn't be able to get the children into the car. I never told them, but they were probably right about that at least.

The following weeks were a time of intense grief for me with the reports that filtered to us from the agency. These reports only compounded my sorrow. Sweet Father, once again Your grace was sufficient (II Corinthians 12:9), and You had big plans just around the corner.

Spring rolled into summer. I was so discouraged and disheartened. On June 4, 1993, I penned this entry in my journal:

Lord, I guess I might as well say it. I'm discouraged about the Hispanic kids. Last night before bed, I asked if You wanted to tell me anything or was there anything I needed to do. All through the night I kept hearing Isaiah 30:20. "And thine ears shall hear a word behind thee saying, This is the way, walk ye in it."

Also You said in Psalm 32:8,

"I will instruct thee and teach thee in the way which thou shall go."

Thank You, Lord, for these reassurances! I love You!

Even in the darkness of my grief and pain, You were able to shine Your light of reassurance on me, but then You are always able.

Less than three weeks later, You spoke again loud and clear. I knew that this was the "word behind me saying this is the way, walk in it" that You had told me of earlier. On June 22, 1993, I wrote a very different entry in my journal:

Lord, I can hardly believe it! "Behold, I will do a new thing: NOW it shall spring forth; shall ye not know it?" (Isaiah 43:19).

You said You would tell me and guide me. Forgive my doubts. I feel like You mean about the kids coming...
   Oh God -- they're coming! They're coming! I can scarcely believe it!

Father, when You pointed that scripture out so clearly, I knew it was You, but I didn't realize just how soon You meant it would spring forth. In the midst of my excitement and anxieties, You poured Your reassurance into me through Your word. Isaiah 44:2-3,

". . . the Lord that made thee. . . will help thee; Fear not. . . My servant. . . whom I have chosen. . . I will pour My Spirit upon thy seed, and My blessing upon thine offspring."

Then You continued with Isaiah 44:7-8:

"And who, as I, shall call, and shall declare it, and set it in order for Me. . . and the things that are coming and shall come let them show unto them. Fear not, neither be afraid: have not I told thee for that time and have declared it?"

Oh yes, You did sweet Father! Oh yes, You did! There is no other God like You! You are magnificently wonderful! You told me more than a year earlier that five Hispanic children were coming. Then You said, "Now it shall spring forth" and two days later it did!

I remember it so well. It was Thursday, June 24, 1993. A friend of mine who also had a heart for adoptions, called me panting and out of breath. She had called the adoption headquarters in Atlanta asking about a Chinese sibling group of three. Those children had already been placed, but the agency had a sibling group of five Hispanic children. Would she consider those? My friend jokingly laughed. She declined because her husband would strangle her if she even mentioned getting that many. He wouldn't have really. His heart is as big as Billy's. Anyway she ended her phone conversation and is in the shower when all of a sudden the thought hit her brain, "Oh my gosh, five Hispanic children! Bonnie's been looking for five Hispanic kids for over a year!" She jumps out of the shower and calls me. The sibling group was in north Georgia when I had been looking in Texas. We still laugh about it to this day.

Alex Ray - 11 years old
Given Billy's Middle Name

I called the state office. According to the worker there were five children: a 13 year old girl, an 11 year old boy, a 9 year old boy, and 7 and 6 year old girls. The next day after talking to the children's case worker, our worker said that everything looked really good. The children had no behavior problems and were all good students. The children were in three separate foster homes. The two younger girls were together in one home. The two boys were placed together in another foster home in an adjacent town, while the 13 year old was staying at a friend's home. I couldn't wait to get them all "home" under one roof like siblings belong! That was and still is a pet peeve of mine, Lord. These children have lost so much by the time they come into foster care that all they have left is each other. I hate siblings being separated. It's just so unfair to the children, but alas, life is not fair.

It was agreed that we could now contact the children's worker. We did. He said we could have the children in two weeks. Father, when You say NOW, You mean now! It actually took three weeks instead of two, but even at that it was nothing short of a miracle.

First we were to go visit them, to meet these children that You had told me were ours one year, two months, and nine days prior to us even knowing of their existence. No other god can reveal such things. Oh Father, You are the only true, living God!

I was so excited and yet so calm on the trip to see the children for the first time. Your peace enveloped me, and I was quite pensive, thinking back over the past year. I had to "eat some crow" and apologize to Billy for not listening to him about just waiting for Your direction. I had made us both miserable in my impatience, calling, calling, calling --- frantically searching.

I also thought of how You must have chuckled at my human reasoning. I felt the need for us to learn the basics of Spanish. I assumed (Oh, how I hate that word now!) that Hispanic children would speak Spanish. Not these Hispanic children! Having been in English speaking foster homes for nearly five years, they knew no Spanish and had southern accents to boot! Billy was a long time in letting me live down my foolishness, and even now he still enjoys teasing me about it.

It didn't matter that I'd been wrong, that they were not in Texas. Nothing mattered because I was about to finally meet our five Hispanic children . . .

Your Expectant Daughter,
Bonnie

Weston Cordel - 9 years old
--Chose his middle name after his hero,
Cordel Walker on Texas Ranger

Chapter Seven

The Springing Forth . . . God's Way

Father,

Words cannot express what it's like seeing a child -- your very own child -- for the first time. It was wonderful! After having waited for more than a year, we were finally introduced to the five Hispanic children that You showed me in a dream.

There was Esmerelda, age 13. She had long, flowing, raven hair down below her waist and a sweet smile. Alex was the eleven year old boy. He was lean and lanky and wore glasses. He was especially eager to make a good impression. Sugel (later called Weston) was an adorable nine year old. He was "Mr. Clown" and happy-go-lucky all rolled into one. Diana, at age seven, was the fearful one. She literally crawled under the table as we entered the room. She was so precious, and even then I knew that Your love could heal her. Pamela was the baby at six years old. She was a beautiful child with a winning smile. I was so filled with love that I thought I would explode for the sheer joy of it. We talked chit-chat for a while, and I drew some pictures on a chalkboard for the children. Then we took the children to get an ice cream. What a delightful time we had! Before we knew it, it was time to return to the office. Foster parents were waiting, and I could barely stand it. I so wanted to load the kids up and carry them home with us. But I could wait a couple more weeks -- I'd have to!

On the trip home Billy and I were both extremely quite. Each of us were processing all the events and emotions of the day. Then Billy asked, "Well, what do you think?" My reply was, "I believe that they are our children." He replied, "I do, too."

We contacted the children's worker the next day and assured them that yes, after meeting the children, we were still definitely interested. Well, there was one small snag. Esmerelda, called Mary, had given up all hope of ever getting to be adopted with her four siblings. They had been in foster care over five years. She had made plans to be adopted by her best friend's parents. Were we still interested in the four younger children? Of course! Our answer was yes, but it troubled me more than Billy because You had said "five." Then You gave me peace. If we had of only been looking for a sibling group of four, we wouldn't have found this group. We both knew in our hearts that these were our children.

The children's worker really wanted Mary to come with the other children, so he convinced her to at least come for a visit with her siblings. Ten days later they spent the weekend with us. We had a wonderful time introducing them to their new brother and five new sisters. Mary said everything went so smoothly. She thought that it was because of me, but I know that it was because of You. That Monday when I took them back to their foster homes, Pamela and Diana, especially Diana, wanted to come back with me. They had been praying for years with the foster parents for a Christian family to adopt them. You answer prayers!

On July 19, 1993, I went to pick up our children and bring them home. Everyone was excited and nervous. Sugel (Weston) was the one who cried about leaving. I had been expecting Diana and Pamela to cry. It never occurred to me that it would be Weston. He didn't misbehave; he was just sad. But Lord, it's such a good thing for them to have had someone to love enough to cry for. We've brought some children home that never cried for anyone. Now, that's really sad. But sadness definitely wasn't the dominating emotion of the day. We were ecstatic and constantly praised Your name. The following morning I wrote this in my journal:

Dear Lord,

Thank You! They're here! Thank You! Thank You! Glory, Glory, Glory -- Lord God, Almighty! Thank You!

Lord, this morning when I opened Your word to Isaiah 28:29, "This also cometh forth from the Lord of hosts, which is wonderful in counsel and excellent in working!" Well, Father, You certainly had been excellent in working.

Speaking of sadness, though, Lord, I felt so sorry for Mary. Thirteen is such a young age to be faced with such an enormous decision. The worker kept pressuring her to come. So because of her foster mom needing a month's rest, Mary agreed to a three week trial visit. I remember her weeping and weeping asking me what was she supposed to do. Father, sometimes state agencies aren't too bright. No thirteen year old should be forced to choose between everything in life that's familiar and her biological siblings. Even in the craziness of it, You reigned. She celebrated her 14th birthday during those three weeks, and she also accepted You as her Savior. She was baptized in the pool in our back yard. You truly work all things for our good (Romans 8:28).

At the end of the three weeks, she went back to the foster parents who planned to adopt her. We assured her if she ever changed her mind that our home was open to her.

In the meantime, You were absolutely astounding me! I had braced myself to be tired. We were nearly doubling the number of children in our home, but it was as if You carried me on eagles' wings. Everything was effortless and miraculous. I felt as if my feet never even touched the ground. You literally were doing the work through me. It was glorious!

The kids had been with us nearly a month when Diana came up to my recliner one day. She laid her head over on me and said, "I love you." Then she stood up and asked, "Am I going to stay here forever?" I assured her that she sure was, at least until she married. She replied, "That's good! I like it here!" Father, she's the one that had suffered the most abuse and yet within a month's time You had already started bridging the gap between brokenness and complete healing. You are truly an awesome God!

Diana Jean - 7 years old
Named after her new Mama

We had prayerfully considered middle names for the children. Alex, now our oldest son, got Billy's middle name -- becoming Alex Ray. Diana would carry my middle name -- Diana Jean. Pamela, prettier than any rose You've ever seen, would be Pamela Rose. She told everyone her new middle name, informing them that mama loves roses! But Sugel, we felt he needed more than just a middle name. We didn't want him teased about his name and apparently that had already happened a lot, because he hated the name Sugel. So, we chose Weston as a first name, and he chose Cordel for his middle one. He loved watching Cordel Walker on the TV show, *Walker Texas Ranger*. That was his hero. So, his name became Weston Cordel. Everyone seemed really pleased about their names, and Lord, I was so pleased and delighted about having these wonderful children. Thank You!

Pamela Rose - 6 years old
"Cause Mama Loves Roses"

Their adoption wouldn't be completed until nearly two years later, but in our hearts and theirs -- they were already Walkers! These four brought our family total up to ten children, which blissfully closed the door on us being allowed to foster because the number of children in our home under the age of ten exceeded state regulations. So with a great sigh of relief and contentment, the foster parent door was closed. As You closed the door on that phase of Your plan, You flung the adoption door wide open! Through it all, I had learned a very valuable lesson. I had learned that it's Your way or no way! Father, lead on . . . lead on!

Your Submitted Daughter,
Bonnie

Chapter Eight

More
Miracles
Coming!

Hello Father,

I have realized through the years that there are times that You "freeze frame" something to get our attention. It's as if You stop everything momentarily and take a picture in our mind's eye that we never forget. It was that way with Ricky.

On the day that I collected Pamela and Diana from their foster home to bring them home with us, You pointed out their foster brother, little Ricky. I can still see that picture of him -- that blonde-haired little boy who was three years old. Now the last thing on my mind was getting more children. After all, I had yet to get the others home, but there he was with You pointing him out. I should have known that You were up to something.

Ricky had been placed in the foster home with his half-sister. For a few years, they remained together, until the mother's parental rights were terminated. Ricky's half-sister was returned to her biological father. Ricky was left by himself in this wonderful Christian foster home. The Department of Children Services pressured the couple to just adopt Ricky themselves. Oh how their hearts yearned to do just that, but You had other plans. You refused to release them from Your very firm "No!" Ricky was not their child. You had chosen us as his parents, and You'd do whatever it took to see Your plan accomplished.

Adoption Time
Weston (10), Pamela (8), Alex (13) & Diana (9)

We had maintained contact with the foster parents through the years. They had lovingly adopted every Walker child as their personal grandchild. So we'd travel back and forth visiting in each other's homes. I remember one visit in January of

1995. They had been with us for several days, and when they left with Ricky it was really hard. As I walked back into our bedroom, I was fighting to maintain control of my tears. I looked to the spot where his little suitcase had laid for the duration of their visit. The imprint of the suitcase was still on the carpet. Not only was the imprint on the carpet, but love for Ricky was imprinted on our hearts as well. We already knew Your plans. There were others in the state agency who had yet to read the writing on the wall. A long, painful battle ensued. Ricky was Caucasian, healthy, and not yet five. He would make an easy placement for a prospective adoptive family that didn't have any children. After all, weren't we being selfish? We already had 10 children and that was enough for anybody. Lord, I guess it is enough for anyone unless You've said otherwise.

We were only licensed to adopt special needs children. The state began to try to declare that Ricky did not qualify as special needs. Ricky was a crack baby, plus he had Attention Deficit Hyperactive Disorder. We knew he needed the special care that we could give. Not to mention, Pamela and Diana had been his foster sisters since he was placed in the foster home as an infant. They were the only "family" he had left. We were determined that with the help of the Lord that was one loss he would not have to suffer. He had already lost so much.

Father, I have never seen Billy as angry as he was the day the state agency told us that Ricky was too "normal", so we would not be able to adopt him. If he had of been handicapped or mentally retarded then we would have the time and means to parent him since we were qualified for such children. But due to the fact that he was so normal, we had too many children to parent one more little boy in need of a home. Righteous anger welled up within Billy. He was furious! As we approached our truck in the parking lot after leaving that meeting, I started laughing. Billy was still huffed and gruffly asked, "What's so funny? What are you laughing at?" Wiping away the tears of laughter, I explained, "Well, Honey, according to one of the case workers, there seems to have been some concern that adopting all these children is my little red wagon. I think you just cleared up that little misconception." He smiled, and I continued laughing, and You prevailed! Ricky was ours, and You would not let anything or anyone stop Your plan! The poor little fellow had already packed his suitcase three times to come home. Each time the bureaucracy that thought we had too many children reared its ugly head.

While we waited, Ricky celebrated his fifth birthday. His foster parents had lovingly brought him here to let us celebrate with him. I made him a big dump truck cake with M & M's piled high on the back. He loved it, but the parting was becoming more difficult. At one point, he even told his caseworker that if she did not hurry up and get the paperwork done that he was going to walk to Mama Bonnie's! Hey, he only lived four hours away! He believed all things are possible with God (Mark 10:27). He still does!

Summer rolled into fall and still no breakthrough with the paperwork. It broke my heart that I didn't get to take Ricky to his first day of Kindergarten. I knew that he was in good, loving hands, but I wanted him in my hands. On November 21, 1995, with Nehemiah 13:2b-3a, You said, "howbeit, our God turned the curse into a blessing. Now it came to pass!" I knew You were saying Ricky was coming home! So on December 18, You made Your long awaited promise a reality. Ricky got to come home just in time to spend Christmas with us. We were all ecstatic! Father, what a priceless treasure he is to our family. Thank You, Lord. Thank You for making a way when there seemingly was no way. Thank You for moving mountains of paperwork, for rolling away every bureaucratic stone! The battle was not ours; none of our battles are. "For the battle is the Lord's" (I Samuel 17:47). Thank You for being our loving Abba Father that fights our battles for us.

Ricky's arrival was a miracle, but You had another miracle on the way. A miracle of which we didn't even have a clue! Well, that's not quite right. Let me rephrase that. The only clue we had is that on August 12, 1995, with Psalm 21:1-7,

You promised me that You had answered my prayer. Nine months and two days later, I would hold that promise in my arms, but let me back up a few months.

Ricky Jonford's 6th Birthday

In January of 1996, we received a phone call asking could and would we house a young fifteen year old expectant mother, who was only half way through her pregnancy. She needed somewhere to stay. She wanted to give her baby up for adoption to a good family. Were we interested? Interested!?! I had been bombarding Heaven with requests for a baby. Could this really be happening? I was so scared, so excited, and so overcome with Your goodness. I thought I would explode! I had asked for a miracle and here it was. I was ecstatic! The next best thing to carrying my own child was to get to care for the one carrying him.

So, for four and a half months, we nurtured and loved this precious child which was carrying our precious child. A child is exactly what she was. She had never experienced anything like the home life that we enjoy here, and she felt as if she'd been transported into a wonderland. Many were the times that Billy and I longed to be able to keep her and the baby. She was so sweet and loving. We rejoiced like the angels in Heaven (Luke 15:10) the day that she accepted Jesus as her Savior. In the spring, we helped her usher in her sixteenth year with a huge birthday party. She was so overwhelmed that her eyes continually filled with tears.

It was such a blessing to get to care for her. Watching the baby grow, going with her to the doctor visits, we did it all together. We were nearly inseparable. Even now my heart overflows with love for this child who gave us her child to raise for You.

At the first doctor's appointment, while listening to the heartbeat, the doctor said, "There's two in there!" I believed that this confirmed what I had already thought that You had revealed to me. Father, I felt so strongly that You had said there would be twins. I was so sure that I even shared my thoughts with the prayer group at church which was something I normally did not do. I was so immature spiritually that I never allowed for any deviation from what I believed You had said. Lord, I had so much to learn (still do!). It was so confusing to me a couple of weeks later when they did a sonogram which showed only one baby. I was stunned, but I set my face like a flint refusing to even consider anything but what I thought You had spoken to me. I'm so glad that You are so tolerant and longsuffering about our immaturity. You don't get all bent out of shape and frustrated when we don't understand. Thank You, sweet Father, for looking at the desire of our hearts to serve You, instead of brow-beating us because we are just babies. You are such a loving, patient Father.

Later, another sonogram revealed that our precious baby was a boy, but still there was no sign of a twin. Tenaciously, I continued to hold on to my belief that there would be twins. Somehow, some way, God would be true to His word.

Those last few weeks are especially dear in my memory. As our little birth mom's tummy continued to swell, so did her anxieties. Could she really do this? Would she always be fat? Would the baby be okay? I, too, had questions of my own. How would I ever be able to let go of this dear young girl whom I had cherished like a daughter? Would our relationship be awkward once she had the baby? Would the daddy relinquish his rights? Would she change her mind? On and on, the questions would race through my mind. I really learned to trust You more as I walked through this season of my life, didn't I, Lord?

We had chosen the name Gabriel Samuel for the baby -- meaning "God is Great," "God Hears," because You had certainly heard my prayers for another baby. We continually praised You and stood in awe of Your unfailing faithfulness.

I had delayed decorating the crib as long as I could, because I didn't want to make things harder on the birth mom. The day we took out all the baby stuff is forever etched in my memory. She looked in awe at all the clothes and baby items. Then she grabbed and hugged me. With tears in her eyes, she said, "Thank you for taking care of my baby and giving him such a good home." Father, bless her for her wisdom and unselfish love in doing the best thing for the baby.

Our time together was quickly drawing to a close. The week before her due date, as we prepared to head to the doctor, I journaled, "Well, Lord this is our next to the last trip to the doctor's office together."

I had no idea on that Monday morning that our baby's birth was closer than I thought. Upon our arrival at the office, the doctor commenced with the normal check up procedure.

When the measurements of the birth mom's abdomen were taken, there was a considerable decrease from the previous week. First, the doctor thought that maybe this was due to the repositioning of the baby lowering in preparation for his birth. Just as she was about to release us she changed her mind. Suddenly she decided to order a sonogram. Later she told me that "something" just told her to do that. That something was Your precious Holy Spirit. Thank You, Lord, for speaking through Your Spirit. I praise You for saying it loud enough that the doctor heard. The sonogram revealed that the amniotic fluid surrounding the baby was dangerously low. Apparently, the birth mom's water had begun leaking, leaving the baby at great risk for complications. It was a miracle that the bumpy ride on our dirt roads had not killed him. One miracle after another, but You are in the miracle business.

There were no more trips home for us. The birth mom was admitted to the hospital with bed rest until the following morning when labor would be induced. It was the last night that Gabriel's two mama's would spend together. It was such a bittersweet time.

The next day, May 14, 1996, after a short and relatively easy delivery, Gabriel Samuel Walker was born weighing 6 pounds and 12.1 ounces. Billy and I were ecstatic!

I had been allowed to stay in the delivery room during the birthing and experience first hand the glorious miracle of our new little son coming into this world. Father, only You could have planned such a marvelous event. But I was so torn between wanting to rush to Gabriel's side as the nurses cleaned him up or remain at the side of his dear birth mom. That feeling would remain with me until she went home the next day. I finally leaned over and kissed her on the cheek while praising her for a job well done. Then I could not wait any longer.

I went to see our new baby boy. Oh Father, You are gloriously marvelous in all Your ways! As the nurses proceeded with all the normal medical proceedings, I got to assist them in bathing Gabriel. I remember how he latched on to my finger with his tiny little hand. What a precious gift straight from

You!

Eventually, the nurses placed him in a little covered isolete in preparation for his journey to the nursery. As the doctor continued to work with the birth mom, I remember standing there thinking, "Well, now they can finally find the other baby -- the twin." But such was not the case, and I was very confused. Thank goodness that with a new baby, I had lots of other things to think about.

Greyson Tyler, Handsome Little Man

Upon arriving at the nursery, they let me hold Gabriel for the first time. We had informed the nursing staff that I would be breast feeding the baby. Who had ever heard of such a thing? Everyone was astounded and in complete unbelief that an adoptive mom could nurse her baby. That is everyone, except me! You had told me with Isaiah 66:11 that it would be so, and so it was. You cannot lie! The first time he nursed it seemed like a dream, but actually it was just another miracle.

Billy was the beaming "proud papa," and the kids couldn't keep their hands off of their new baby brother when they came to visit that evening. We caused quite a stir at the hospital. A family with eleven children wanting to adopt another baby was not the norm. We definitely stood out as not ordinary, but as long as we're Your peculiar people (I Peter 2:9), I don't mind if people think I'm a little strange. Okay, okay! I don't care if they think I'm a lot strange. You are so funny. I love to laugh with You. I love You, Lord.

The next day the parental rights papers were signed saying that Gabriel was officially ours. I told this sweet young girl that this baby was the best Mother's Day present I had ever received, but having to say good-bye to her was one of the hardest things I've ever done. My mothering heart was so full of love and protectiveness towards her that I could hardly stand it, but Your grace is sufficient in every area. You carried us through our teary good-byes.

Your Emotionally Drained,
but Grateful Daughter,
Bonnie

Chapter Nine

Raging Waters, Spiritual Darkness, And Questions

Dear Abba,

It had been such an emotional roller coaster the past few days that it was taking a toll on my body, but there were more rough waters ahead. The pediatrician was beginning to get concerned about Gabriel not urinating. If he would just urinate, we could go home. We immediately started praying. Thank You, Father, for not answering that prayer. His inability to urinate was only a warning that something else was wrong.

By 7:30 p.m. that Wednesday evening, I was physically and emotionally wiped out. A sweet, angelic nurse allowed me to lay down on a cot in a spare room there at the hospital so that I could be close to Gabriel to nurse him at his feedings. Father, even the timing of my nap was orchestrated by You. All alone, at approximately 11:00 p.m., I faced one of the most frightening times of my life. Except I wasn't alone, was I? You never left me nor forsook me, just like You promised in Hebrews 13:5. You remained ever-present with me.

Close to 11 o'clock a nurse woke me up saying that Gabriel's pediatrician wanted to speak with me. This sweet Christian doctor lovingly informed me that Gabriel needed to be transferred by ambulance to a larger hospital with an extensive neo-natal unit. Gabriel's stomach was distended -- cause unknown! Because the reason for the swelling was undetermined, I'd have to discontinue breastfeeding for now and he'd be placed on IV fluids. Oh God, by the time they had prepared him for the trip he had wires and tubes going in every direction. I've always been kind of freaky about needles, and the thought of Gabriel being stuck with one nauseated me. You held me together, and I managed to follow the ambulance to Macon. The ambulance drivers weren't supposed to let me follow them, but they were concerned about me being on the road at that time of night by myself so they consented. Father, here again You showed up by giving us favor. Your favor would continue to be poured out on us through the entire neo-natal staff and other hospital officials.

Upon arrival at the hospital, in the wee hours of the morning, Gabriel was immediately surrounded by doctors and nurses. After a thorough examination and a battery of tests were ordered, the doctors gave me several possibilities of a diagnosis, but basically we were playing a waiting game.

Some of the tests could not be completed due to the thin linings of Gabriel's intestinal walls. Two days later on Friday, his distended stomach was slowly going down. We were all hopeful.

In the meantime, Billy was holding down the fort at home with the other children. Our church family was such a blessing by helping out with food and in a multitude of other ways. Money was donated to pay for my room there in the hospital so that I could be near Gabriel. I don't know how we would have possibly managed without their help.

The days floated by with me staying in the nursery with Gabriel nearly all day, then retiring to my room late at night and returning early the next morning. I'd talk and sing to him while gently stroking his cheek, arm, or leg. Oh yeah, and I'd pray! I commanded every demon of hell to release their hold in Jesus' name. I read Your word like a starving person. Searching for some answers to all the questions shooting through my brain.

After nearly two weeks, we finally had a diagnosis -- Hurshsprung's disease. The nerve endings on a section of Gabriel's intestines were dead, and he would need surgery to remove the diseased section. A colostomy would be put in place with hopes of later rerouting his intestines for normal bowel movements. Oh Father, at first I was stunned. You helped me realize that the surgery itself was a miracle. Without the surgery, Gabriel would die. So it was a miracle -- just not the kind I'd hoped for.

For two weeks, we had see-sawed back and forth between getting to let Gabriel breastfeed, taking a bottle so his intake amounts could be measured exactly, and being totally dependant on IV fluids for all his nourishment. Now we were looking at several more days of no nursing. I came so close to giving up on the breastfeeding, Lord. The nurses informed me that even a birth mom, having to start and stop breastfeeding as many times as I'd had to, would have a very limited milk supply, but I still persisted. I figured every ounce he got from me would be to his advantage heath-wise. If I had to supplement, so be it. I was determined to do all I could, and I prayed constantly for You to supply my milk flow.

So, at two weeks of age little Gabriel Samuel underwent surgery with no complications. He looked so pitiful with tubes everywhere. It was almost more than I could handle. Josey, bless her heart, nearly fainted when she saw her baby brother right after his surgery. We praised You for a successful surgery and looked forward to finally getting to go home.

On Saturday, June 1, 1996, after two and a half weeks, Gabriel's doctors released him from the hospital. The kids couldn't believe that we were actually home! I couldn't either! I laid our little angelic bundle in the bassinet where he was converged upon by all his brothers and sisters. Thank

You, Father, home at last!

Gabriel Samuel Walker - 4 ½ months old

The days went by in a constant blur of caring for Gabriel. This is normal with a newborn, but the colostomy took an excessive amount of time to prepare and apply. Sometimes it had to be changed several times a day. There was a constant battle trying to control leaks and the odor, but those things weren't what was tormenting my soul. I would have walked over hot coals if that's what it took to care for my precious son. What was torturing me was a question reverberating constantly in my head. "Hath God said?" The devil mercilessly bombarded my mind with that one question.

I had been so sure that You had said twins. What happened? How could I have been so wrong? Then there was the horrifying thought, if I was wrong about the twins, what else was I wrong about? Could I even hear my sweet Father's voice at all? Or was I only imagining it?

The darkness threatened to consume me. One dear couple, who had spent weeks in our home every year, confided to some of our church family that they had never seen me like this before. Of course I was not aware of their concern, all I knew was that the thought of not being able to hear Your voice terrified me more than anything in my entire life.

You tried to shine through the darkness with scripture like Jeremiah 33:3. "Call to Me, and I will answer you, and show you great and mighty things, which you do not know." Then Satan would come again with, "Remember, you were wrong about the twins. Do you really think God's saying that this scripture is just for you? You were wrong once, and what if you're wrong this time, too?"

Sweet Abba, You even sent a message through one of my prayer partners. You said, "Bonnie, stand firm, because of your faith . . . I will be victorious . . . I love you, My child." But still the battle raged. It was as if a cloak of darkness covered my entire spiritual life. Though I caught flickers of light, the darkness definitely was dominating, trying to consume me. In September, after months of being assaulted with the fiery darts of doubt, the devil's relentless tirade continued. If I was so wrong about the twins, then I could be wrong about so much else.

Scary, terrifying thought! Paralyzing thought! I couldn't deal with the fact that I'd misunderstood and been wrong about something that I was so sure about. Maybe there was lots more I had misunderstood.

Now, Father, after much growth, I know to tell Satan to take a flying leap back to where he came from in Jesus' name. I praise You, God, for spiritual revelation of how to war in the spirit realm. I love the fact that Your word is true, and what Satan intended for evil You have used to save many people (Genesis 50:20) from the torture that I went through. If You had not allowed this attack, I might never have learned about spiritual warfare. I might never have learned how to resist the devil so that he has to flee from me (James 4:7) in the mighty name of Your Son, Jesus. It was a lesson that has proven invaluable in bringing healing to these precious children and many others besides. I praise You, Father, for the process, that dark spiritual tunnel, that taught me so much and which You used to bring such a wealth of revelation to my soul. The pain was well worth the gain. It is the same way with every trial that you allow to touch our lives. You never allow anything to touch us that is not for our good and Your glory (Romans 8:28). You are such a good God! I love You!

I've learned now that I can even be wrong about what I think You're saying, and it's not the end of the world. Satan will never again be able to torture me with the thought of You not talking to me or me being incapable of hearing Your sweet voice. Hallelujah!

After this major spiritual battle was won, You shared a secret through a dream. By this time, it was September of 1996. (I mention the month for a specific reason.) In the dream, a blonde-haired baby boy was lying on a little table directly in front of me, close to me. Another black haired baby boy was far off in the distance, far from me a long way off. They were both my babies, and I knew by the dream that they both belonged to me. My 'opposite' twins! I had heard correctly about the twins! I had just put the wrong interpretation and application to the revelation You had given me. Not only that, but it would be nearly three years before I'd see the manifestation and fulfillment of the promise. But Father, what You say will and does come to pass! And I praise You!

In the meantime, You carried our little angel Gabriel through on angels' wings. In October his corrective surgery for rerouting the colostomy was a complete success. He was only five and a half months old, but You had given me a scripture so that I wouldn't worry. Psalm 118:17, 23, "I (Gabriel) shall not die, but live, and declare the works of the Lord." Verse 23, "The Lord has done this, and it is marvelous in our eyes," was our glad shout of victory! Thank You, Father, for Your words of truth, for growth, and for Your fresh mercies each morning (Lamentations 3:23). I love You!

Your Wiser Daughter,
Bonnie

Chapter Ten

Peace
and
More

Well Father,

Just prior to Gabriel's surgery at the end of October, we celebrated a double adoption. On October 2, 1996, Ricky and Gabriel became legal members of our family. I will not say official members, Father, because officially we feel the kids are ours from the first day You tell us that they are ours.

That put us up to twelve, an even dozen. Whoever says, "Cheaper by the dozen!" hasn't seen our grocery bill. Nevertheless, we were very blessed. You let us take a breather for a couple of years. It was a wonderful time of growth and contentment in You. The contentment was new for me. I had been almost driven by an ever present yearning of more children, the urge to help more kids. During this time, You helped me grow up in You to the place that I was no longer trying to work Your plan for You. I guess what really happened is that You grew up in my eyes as I began to see just how big a God You truly are! It was as if You were saying, "Finally, I believe the girl has got it!" It took long enough, huh? I relinquished the reins of my life to You, being truly content with the number of children You had blessed Billy and myself with. If You wanted more, that was fine; if You didn't, that was fine, too.

It is not until hindsight that I can see the place You wanted me all along. Now, You could really work through our lives. In the meantime, You started us into home schooling. By the start of the third year, You had provided us a classroom in the backyard. Having the kids here all the time was another major blessing. It was the strangest thing. I felt as if someone had given my children back to me, and I hadn't even realized that I felt like someone or something had taken them away.

In the fall of 1998 (with our four oldest having moved out to various walks of life: marriage, college, etc.), You began the familiar tugging again. More children, Lord? Your reply was a resounding, "Yes!" We didn't realize at the time just how big of a "yes" You meant.

This time we began the search led by the Holy Spirit. Through a friend, a connection with a Texas case worker in Corpus Christi was established. Once again we were looking for a Hispanic sibling group. We began the long tedious process of updating our home study.

When the worker mailed us a picture of a sibling group of four, my heart responded with a sense of knowing that they were ours. Billy agreed to proceed full speed ahead. It wasn't until February 22, 1999, that we received official word from the case worker confirming what I already believed in my heart to be true. Not only had You chosen and approved us as these children's parents, but the state of Texas confirmed it by agreeing with Your choice. Four more children were on the way! We rejoiced exceedingly! You were blessing us with a nine year old girl, followed by a seven year old boy, a five year old girl, and a two year old boy.

I worried our poor case worker half to death. I was so impatient to see our new little ones. They had been through so much. The two oldest had been in numerous foster homes for nearly six and a half years. The younger two were crack babies, so the state placed them immediately in foster care at their births. When little Adam was born, he was in such bad shape that he died and had to be resuscitated. You are a merciful God! The doctor said that he almost didn't make it, but You had a plan that Satan couldn't stop. Thank You, Lord!

Sweet Anna Abigail - 11 years old

The missing piece of the puzzle about the promise of twins finally fell into place when we were told Adam's birthday. Bringing with it complete understanding of the dream of the baby up close to me and the dark haired baby far away. The same month that You told me of the dark haired baby far away is the very month in which Adam was born -- September! You are amazing. I was about to see the fulfillment of the promise of twins that You'd told me of two years earlier. It is incredible to watch You work.

Another thing, for which I was grateful, is that for most of their lives this sibling group had at least been in the same foster home. For so many large sibling groups, that is not the case. These four had been separated a few times for a few months, but for the most part You had kept them together. Hallelujah!

March 1, 1999, still holds a very sweet memory for me. We were finally allowed to call the children. I spoke with Anna, the oldest, asking her, "Do you know who this is?" Her reply, "My new Mom!" I laughed through my tears of joy. We continued to keep in contact with the children until March 5, when we traveled to Texas to see them for the first time. We met at the foster parents' home. The children were absolutely adorable. Our hearts were even more captivated with Your love for these precious little ones. We had a wonderful weekend with the children: playing with the gifts we'd brought them, playing games, baking cookies, walking on the beach, and just getting to know each other.

When we returned the children to their foster parents, the two girls cried wanting to come home with us right then. David hid behind a mask of indifference pretending to be absorbed in a video game. Adam seemed totally oblivious to the whole proceeding. We promised them that we really wanted them. We tried to reassure them that in a couple of weeks the case worker would bring them home to us. For children who had been lied to most of their lives, our words fell on deaf ears. Only time would prove the truth to them. I kept a brave face in front of them, but as we pulled away from the house the flood gates opened as tears cascaded down my cheeks. Billy was so sweet and considerate. He soothed me with reassuring words just as we had tried to soothe the kids.

David, Showing Off His Prized Egg

Back at home, on March 12, You reassured me even more with Ezekiel 36:8b -- "for they are soon to come home." It could not be soon enough for me. I had left my four babies in Texas thousands of miles away. It was torture on my mothering heart waiting as paperwork was shuffled back and forth between Georgia and Texas. Finally everything was in order, and the big day was set for them to fly home.

Bethany Nicole - So Loving!
6 years old

Anna Abigail (9), David Joseph (7), Bethany Nicole (5), and Adam Nathaniel (2) arrived here in Georgia on March 29, 1999, with smiles, laughter, and tears of joy to be with their new family. There were tears in our eyes, too. Tears of gratitude to be chosen to love these precious souls You had entrusted to our care. Oh, dear Father, help us to be faithful to Your task.

Gabriel's 'opposite twin', Adam, was finally home. With Gabriel's fair complexion, blonde hair, and blue eyes next to Adam's dark complexion, black hair, and dark brown eyes, they looked nothing alike. Adam was such an independent little man, while Gabriel was used to brothers and sisters doting on him hand and foot. Yet with looks and personalities so completely opposite, there was an immediate bond between them just like twins. If one fell down the other one would cry. It was amazing to watch their interaction with each other. You laid everyone's fears to rest about Gabriel being jealous. He never once acted jealous. He was just thrilled to have his brother home.

Adam Nathaniel
Happy 3rd Birthday!

Things went smoothly. The kids suffered very little culture shock. The fourteen of us snuggled cozily in the same 2,400 square foot home. We barely noticed the tight quarters except when the hot water ran out, and two of us still needed a bath. Or on heavy wash days, when there would be twelve or more loads of laundry to get washed. We had our eyes on more eternal things. One morning Anna asked, "Why didn't anyone in Texas tell us about Jesus?" You'll have to answer that one for her, Lord. I am sure that I don't know.

Your Contented Daughter,
Bonnie

Chapter Eleven

Miracles Manifesting

Hello Sweet Father,

That spring was a sweet, precious time. I was tired, but so very content. At least I was content, until September rolled around. Then some very unusual and unique (yet, very familiar to me) things began to happen. I had long since learned that there's more than one way to be pregnant. As ridiculous as it may sound to others, Lord, I know you know what I mean. Each time, before children came, I would just know that in the spirit I was pregnant. Cravings, weepy, unexplainable nesting urges, and clingy younger children! Gabriel and Adam all of a sudden turned into mama's boys. I couldn't move without one or both of them wanting me to hold them. I knew what was coming, but unlike with a natural pregnancy I didn't know the when, from what direction, the number of children, or their ages. I just knew that I was pregnant -- again!

Saturday, September 18, 1999, I felt extremely weepy, but

with missionary friends staying with us, I tried to act normal (whatever that is). By the time we had lunch, I finally excused myself with the comment that I had to go see what You wanted. I knelt on the floor in our bedroom and let the tears fall. I just kept crying before You. Then all of a sudden I cried out, "God, please take care of that Hispanic baby boy!" Then I froze in stunned silence while the thought ricocheted inside my brain. What Hispanic baby boy? I began to intercede again asking You to guard and protect him. I asked that You keep Your heavenly angels stationed around him. After about thirty minutes, peace settled over me. I knew my intercession was complete, at least for now. Still my question was unanswered. What Hispanic baby boy?

Upon sharing the experience, a friend suggested that perhaps Anna, David, Bethany, and Adam's birth mom had had another baby. I agreed to call our case worker on Monday to check out the possibility. Late that afternoon, once again I was overcome with the urgency to pray for the baby's safety.

Monday came, and I contacted our case worker in Texas. I explained what had happened and questioned her about the possibility of the birth mom being pregnant again. She was more than a little upset with me, and I believe she thought I was more than a little crazy. When You said Your children are to be a strange and peculiar people (I Peter 2:9), You might should have jotted down a footnote: People will think you are crazy! It is comfort to my soul that they thought my big brother, Jesus, was crazy, too. I love laughing and teasing with You, my Lord! You are wonderful! But let me get back to my story.

On Monday, exactly two weeks later, at 3:15 p.m., I recorded this entry in my journal:

I called a friend asking her to pray because I felt 'anticipatory.' (My word for the feeling I get when I feel that something big is about to happen. Lord, I had no idea just how big, but You did.) My friend asked, "So you

don't feel like you are supposed to go to Texas to finalize the adoption?" I was scheduled to fly out the next day, October 5th. I said, "No, it's not that. It's more like when I get out there they are going to show me a picture of some kids and say these are yours."

I had no idea just how accurate that prophesy was, but I was about to find out! Shortly, after I journaled that conversation, I received a phone call from our worker in Texas. She sounded terribly distraught. Not too calmly, she told me to get to another phone so that no one could hear our conversation. My first thought was, oh great, someone forgot to cross some 't' or dot an 'i' with the adoption paperwork so that we would be unable to finalize the adoption on Wednesday. Followed quickly by my second thought, here I am with plane tickets that I can't use, but You had another surprise!

As I picked up the receiver of our bedroom phone, our case worker began exclaiming quite loudly, "That woman had a baby! That woman had a baby! How did you know she was pregnant? We didn't even know!" She was referring to my phone call two weeks prior. What an awesome testimony to the fact that You speak to Your children. Your word in Amos 3:7 is true, "Surely the Lord God will do nothing, but He revealed His secret unto His servants. . .". Her next question thrilled me. Would we be interested in adopting him also? Oh God, You are so awesome! Your timing is so infinitely perfect. Flying to Texas the following day, I experienced such a spirit of humbleness. All I could think of was "How BIG is God?". That night in the hotel room, before I went to sleep, You said with Exodus 16:7, "And in the morning, then ye shall see the glory of the Lord!" I did Lord; it was 'glory, glory, glory' all day long!

The next day October 6, 1999, I finalized our adoption on Anna and her siblings. I got so teary-eyed during the proceedings. Everyone was congratulating me when someone said something about the baby. The judge asked, "There's another one?" He refused to have the case removed from his court.

He'd dealt with the kid's birth mom for years, so he had an invested interest in this case. The judge didn't want this baby to get lost in paperwork. He wanted everything expedited. This was an absolute miracle! The case worker and lawyers nearly fainted. They had never seen nor heard of anything like it. The whole Corpus Children Protective Services unit was standing on their head. You are so awesome! The entire trip You anointed us with such favor. I told my missionary friend who had made the trip with me that I felt as if You were shining this huge spotlight on me saying, "Be nice to this lady!" It was almost unbelievable!

The next event was more thrilling than what had happened in the courtroom. I was taken to the hospital's neo-natal unit to be introduced to our new son. The day before, Billy had chosen the name Joel, meaning "Jehovah is God." After I got to Texas, You added Isaac which means 'laughter.' Joel Isaac Walker had been born on Sunday, October 3, 1999, weighing 8 pounds 2 ounces. He was absolutely beautiful with a head full of jet black hair. My heart exploded with love. He'd been diagnosed cocaine positive at birth with a grade three bleeder on his brain. I didn't care what the doctors said; I knew he was our baby. We took pictures, loved on him, fed him, and changed his diaper--and we prayed! You performed a miracle!

Lord, You know that any medical personnel will quickly tell you that a grade three brain bleeder is serious business. We stood there the next morning quite amused as a very puzzled doctor tried to explain the miraculous. He couldn't figure out what was wrong. He thought that someone must have made a mistake, because the CT of Joel's brain from that morning appeared perfectly normal. He scratched his head telling us that a grade one bleeder might seal itself off. It is even possible for a grade two bleeder to seal off without leaving any residue. With a grade three bleeder, the doctor said it was not possible. Well, listen up doc. I have news for you. With my God, "all things are possible" (Matthew 19:26)! I left out of the NICU singing, "I'm under the Blood of the Lamb. I'm safe and secure from the enemy's plan. No weapon formed against me will stand. I'm under the Blood of the Lamb."

I returned home praying for mountains of paperwork to be moved so that Joel could come home quickly. They kept Joel in the hospital several days, running repeated cat-scans, wasting the state's money, trying to understand a miracle. Oh, Glorious, Father, Hallelujah! You are awesome! You even placed Joel in a Christian foster home, and from what I was told those are few and far between in Corpus Christi. Knowing that he was with part of Your family made the wait easier, but it was a long five and a half weeks.

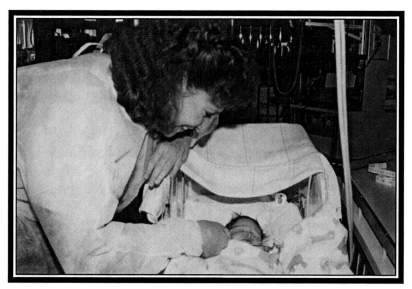

Bonnie's 1st Visit with Baby Joel in Neonatal Unit

On November the tenth, You brought our precious baby boy home. We were ecstatic. The children were so funny. They thought the only thing wrong with having a baby brother was that there was only one of him to pass around.

Joel was home. You had healed his brain of the grade three bleeder. He still suffered from the ravages of the drugs that were in his system at birth. He was easily irritated with spells of excessive crying and fretfulness. There is some long name for it that I cannot remember right now, but it was basically withdrawal symptoms. I prayed and laid hands on him and prayed some more. Wondering, Father, why would You not hear my plea and heal this baby? He became highly agitated in the doctor's office during a checkup one day. His doctor wanted to put him on the medicine to counteract the withdrawals. I told her no, but I did come home and discuss it some more with Billy. Billy wanted to know if he would outgrow it. I relayed what the doctor had said. Usually within six months the drugs will wear out of the infant's system. We decided to tough it out, but I still continued my relentless praying. It was during this time that You were really working on me about any pride in my life. And I was so proud of my baby boy -- drug addicted, a misplaced ear, a cyst on one side of his head, a bald spot on the other side, and the middle toe on his right foot nearly invisible because the toes on either side overlapped it -- but to me he was beautiful beyond measure, and I wanted to show him off to the world.

Then the revelation came. It was a typical Sunday morning. Everyone was trying to get ready for church, and as usual, with anything unusual going on, Joel began to get irritated. I tried everything to calm him. This morning nothing worked. I finally gave up in frustration and put him back to bed which was the only way to get him settled down. Billy and the children went on to church. I felt so sorry for myself. I remember walking into our bedroom and saying to You, "Lord, I cannot even take him to church and . . . and . . . show him off." We wonder why You allow trials in our life? It is in the midst of trials that we see truth. Halfway through that statement You had spotlighted the problem. Pride, my sin of pride. I collapsed on my knees into a heap of heart wrenching tears and sobs. I confessed my sin to You, and I cried to a loving Father, "Oh God, please don't punish my baby because of my sin." I knew You could heal, that Your desire was to heal, but I also knew Your Word. You will not hear nor answer my prayer *"if I regard iniquity in my heart"* (Psalm 66:18). You hate pride. I called out to Heaven in repentance, and You delivered my baby. He had been home ten days when You set him free. Words cannot describe the love in my heart for You. I praise You.

Adoption Bliss! Adam (3), David (8), Anna (10) & Bethany (6)

When Joel got up that evening, he got up a new baby. The change was so obvious that the next day I casually asked the lady that was helping me home-school that year if she had noticed anything different about Joel. She stood there a few seconds, watching him in the cradle, and then she exclaimed, "He's peaceful!" All glory to You, Father—all praise and glory to Your Holy Name! You truly are a miraculous God, a loving Father, the Great Physician, and I adore You!"

Your Miraculously Amazed Daughter,
Bonnie

Chapter Twelve

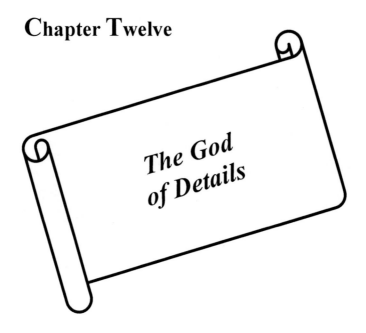

The God of Details

Dearest Abba,

You truly are a Promise Keeper. Our family now numbered seventeen children. Thirteen of them at home with four grown and on their own, plus Billy and myself, we totaled out at nineteen. But You weren't finished yet. February 19, 2000, I dreamed that I got three tiny brown biddies. Here we go again! I knew the biddies represented children. It wasn't the first time in figurative dream language that You had used biddies to symbolize children.

In April, our case worker in Texas mailed us a picture of three little girls, along with a brief description of their lives. We would be dealing with the painful issues of abandonment and neglect, on the streets without a home, going all day without food -- all the normal things we so take for granted. Oh Father, it breaks my heart to know how all our children have suffered, and I know that it breaks Yours. Sometimes I question why they couldn't have come home sooner, but You are sovereign, and Your grace is sufficient. They have so many wounds which need Your healing touch. I praise You, God, that You are a God who "will restore. . . the years that the locust hath eaten" (Joel 2:25). Father, You know that I pray for our children who are not home yet, but I am so grateful I didn't know the details then as I do now. There is only so much that a mother's heart can handle! Knowing it now is hard enough when they're safe. They are snuggled in their comfortable beds, sleeping peacefully after a good supper, followed by precious prayers, and lots of hugs and kisses. Now I can handle it, when I can reach out and touch them and hug them. Oh, thank You, Jesus, that even as You reveal Your will, I still "see through a glass darkly" (I Corinthians 13:12) the things that would torment my soul. But enough sadness, enough tears . . .

These three captured our hearts just like You intended, and a very unusual thing happened. Billy usually says to wait until we know for sure they're coming before we decide on their new names. You know this name changing business used to really bother me until You reminded me that all throughout the Bible when people would come into Your presence, You would change their names. So, hey, we are just imitating our Father. You are so wonderful! But getting back to what happened, I felt in my spirit that You said the girls would be Faith, Hope, and Charity. But like I said, Billy usually doesn't want to discuss names until we have official word from the state's social services that the children are actually coming here. When I told Billy what I felt You had said, he replied, "That's fine, but let those be their middle names, not the names they will be called." He thought that would be a little too cute. You and I both know this was so unlike my dear Mr. Wait and See. So after more prayer, Charity Ruth, Rebekah Hope, and Lydia Faith were decided upon. Now our caseworker had told us that the staffing (the big event where caseworkers get together and decide the fate of Your little ones' lives, choosing between three or four families which family they believe will provide the best home) would be sometime in June or July, and here we were with a picture and new names. Father, I don't know if I can ever tell this story where it will make sense to anyone else besides You and me. On April 28 of 2000 (which was the previous April), I was thinking, I wish I knew for sure before the staffing if the three girls were the ones we were getting. Then You said, "Ecclesiastes 6:10," which reads, "Whatever exists has already been named. . .[!]" Now, to no one else would it make any sense, but I knew You were saying to me that You had already named these as our children. I wrote in my journal "You are so neat!" You are! But what made it even more special is that I didn't consciously stop and ask You. I was just pondering on these thoughts, and You answered, just like Your Word says, "And it shall come to pass that, before they call, I will answer" (Isaiah 65:24). You alone are a God capable of such awesomeness. Oh, I praise You, Lord! I praise You!

So, with Your scripture confirmation, I allowed something I had never allowed before and probably won't allow again. I let our children announce that they were getting three new sisters. Wow, leap of faith! Well, June and July rolled over with social services doing their normal snail's crawl pace and eventually setting the staffing for August 11, 2000. My caseworker kept telling me that she did not believe we would get the girls, but I believed on, hoping against all hope. She questioned me, "Are you sure?" I replied, "Well, let me put it to you this way. I've been wrong before, so I won't say 100% for sure, but I'm way on up in the 98-99% sure!"

Well, August 11th rolled around, and the staffing came and went deciding that "our" girls would be placed with an adoptive family in Houston. I did not find out until January of the following year that the decision was not made on which home was the best, but it was based on the fact that it would be cheaper to fly them to Houston than all the way to Georgia! I cried, grieved, put their little picture in a drawer, and admitted that, "Well, God, I missed You big time on this one! Unless there is an adoption disruption (where the prospective adoptive parents back out and decide they do not want to adopt these kids after all), then You have closed this door." But I kept their picture in the drawer, and every time I opened the drawer my heart felt the pain of the piercing loss. My girls? But God? I thought. I was so sure--I thought I heard You say.

Hearing Your voice more clearly had been my prayer focus for several months. Even though it seemed as if I'd missed You about the girls, You were about to reveal that You definitely are a God of details, and that You speak very clearly to Your children. I remember during this time reminding You about Noah and Moses and how You spoke with them in detail. You told them so many cubits this way and that for building the Ark and the tabernacle. I bombarded Heaven for months, crying out to You to please talk to me specifically with exact details. My passion was to hear Your voice clearly.

Well, on the morning of June 22, 2000, You spoke through Genesis 30:24 saying that You would add to us another son and his name was Joseph. I dated the scripture in the margin of my Bible and recorded it in my journal. I had finally learned to patiently wait for the fulfillment of whatever You said. I guess, truthfully, I should say I had learned to be "more" patient during the waiting.

That fall, on September 19, I received a phone call from the private adoption agency here in Georgia who had monitored the placement of the sibling group from Texas. This agency, which primarily deals with infant adoptions, was in a unique situation. Our worker explained that they had custody of a seven year old little boy who needed temporary foster care. They had become involved several months prior when the desperate birth mom had called the agency crying out for help. Parental rights were terminated, and Chuck (as he was called) was placed in one of the agency's foster homes. Later he was moved to an adoptive home, but had now experienced another heart-wrenching rejection—an adoption disruption! A terrible situation where a prospective adoptive family decides not to finalize on an adoption for various reasons. So the agency needed another foster home and fast!

Five Musketeers!
Weston (16, is trying to figure out what Alex (18) thinks
is so funny. Pamela (13), Katrina (16) and Diana (14)
are grinning in the background.

I hated to tell our worker no, but I hated fostering worse than I hated telling her no. Lord, I remember saying to her, "I don't do fostering so well, but we'll take him. We'll adopt him." I told her that the fostering scared me. She hesitated, undecided. With the amount of rejection the little fellow had already suffered, they believed he didn't need to be placed with so many siblings. Their opinion was that he needed more one-on-one attention, but she would run it by the director. In the meantime, I spoke with Billy. He felt the same way I did about wanting to adopt the little boy. The only difference being that if the agency said no, he thought we should still help them out with fostering him. The agency had been so marvelous in working with us on our Texas adoptions that Billy felt that we should bless them in return.

Phone calls flew back and forth all afternoon between us and the caseworker. A little after eleven o'clock that night, we had one final conversation. My worker said to pray that the director would hear from You, because she would do whatever You said. I told her that in Proverbs 21:1, it says that You turn the heart of the king (the agency director) like You turn the river the way You want it to go. That was my prayer. I also let her know that we were going on a field trip with a home school group the following day, so it would be that afternoon before she could reach me.

We returned home around 1:30 p.m. and I immediately called the agency. Our worker said that she had been praying that You would tell me to call. The agency director had walked into the office at 9:00 a.m. and said, "He's going to the Walker's!" Wow! You go, God! How simple a thing for You to turn the river! The worker wanted to bring Chuck to the house that afternoon around five. Could we be ready? Was that okay? We began the mad dash to get his bed, chest of drawers, and closet space ready. Lord, that was the fastest fruit-basket turnover we had ever accomplished!

So that Wednesday afternoon, on September 20, 2000, our new son arrived with blonde hair and the most breathtaking pale blue eyes. He was terribly frightened and visibly trembling. Because of his past wounds, he had such a fear of being rejected once again. Oh, but Father, You had planned all along to remove that fear. You had a surprise in store, not just for him, but for me as well. After all the introductions, some play time, supper followed with baths, and bedtime which ran later than normal due to the special occasion. I collapsed into the recliner - tired, but happy!

It was after 11:00 p.m., but I decided to make good use of the time by sorting through some of Chuck's paperwork. When I came across his birth certificate, tears sprang into my eyes, and I began to weep. Chuck's middle name was Joseph! I cried and cried at the clarity with which You had spoken months earlier, telling me You would add to us a son named Joseph! That was only a portion of the revelation. You had an even greater confirmation planned for the following morning. As I went to sleep that night, my heart sang with praises of Your loving kindness in speaking to me, Your child.

The next day I put in to find the scripture that I'd marked back during the summer that You had given to me proclaiming Your promise of our son named Joseph. There it was: Genesis 30:24, with June 22, 2000 dated next to it. Then I continued sorting Joseph's paperwork. The agency had written a brief history of their involvement in Joseph's life. As I started to read it, I was absolutely stunned! It began with the statement:

"Birth mom contacted agency on the morning of June 22, 2000 . . ."

Joseph (9) & Jumper

I started bawling! On the exact same day and time that the birth mom had called the agency asking for help, You told me that You were giving us a son named Joseph!

I made the mistake of calling the agency before I regained my composure. I was almost incoherent because I was crying so hard. It scared the worker. She thought Joseph had ran away or something horrible had happened. I began to reassure her: "No! No! You misunderstand. These are happy tears. In case anyone woke up this morning wondering if you made the right decision about placing Joseph in a home with so many other children, I just wanted to let you know what God had to say about it!" Then I shared what You had revealed with scripture, dates, names, and timing. There was no doubt in anyone's mind that Joseph was finally home!

It was so glorious getting to share with our new son all that You had said and done. Such peace and joy washed over him, transforming his entire countenance. There would be no more rejection for Joseph. No more changing homes. He was home to stay - the God of the universe had spoken! One of my prayer partners explained it this way: she said that Joseph had a call on his life, and that You needed him here to fulfill that call. I believe that is even more true than we realize.

Oh God, how wonderful you are! I asked for details desiring to hear Your voice. You answered the cry of my heart. While at the same time, You began the healing process of restoration to one seven year old little boy's wounded heart. You are truly a multifaceted God knowing the end from the beginning. And I love You!

Your Delighted Daughter,
Bonnie

Chapter Thirteen

The Promise Keeper

Dear Father,

So, there we were, fourteen kids in four bedrooms, and still You were stirring our hearts once again. There were more children that You wanted to bring home. Lord, You said, "Enlarge your house; build an addition; spread out your home! For you will soon be bursting at the seams" (Isaiah 54:2-3a). I remember Billy laughing and saying, "I thought we already were!"

After You had sent Joseph to us, I could see Your reasoning as to why we had not got the three girls in Texas back in August. Still their little picture remained in the top drawer of our chest of drawers. Why couldn't I throw it away? At the time I didn't understand, but now I know why. You wouldn't let me close the door because You weren't through with that situation yet. You hadn't said the final word yet, but You were about to.

In January, our Texas case worker casually mentioned that

the girls' adoption wasn't working out. The other family could not handle the strain of parenting these three needy little girls. They did not have the necessary parenting skills, so after some inappropriate discipline of the girls (sitting them outside at night in the cold for time out and other incidents), the state stepped in again and rescued "our" girls. These precious children were facing another rejection, another upheaval, and more pain. But You had a plan, and You didn't care what the plane tickets would cost. So on January 31st, Tina, our adoption worker, called asking us if we wanted the girls. Did we want our girls? Of course! Yes, we would take them!

So preparation and juggling started all over again. I honestly can't remember how many different beds and bedrooms any given child has had, but that's okay. Your promise in Colossians 3:23-24 makes it all worth while. "Whatever you do, do it heartily, as to the Lord . . . Knowing that from the Lord you will receive the reward of the inheritance, for you serve the Lord Christ." We have tried so hard to instill that principle into these children. Lord, bless them for their willingness to give "as unto the Lord!" Father, bless them all. They are truly doing it unto the least of these Your other children, so they are doing it unto You. What amazes me is the lack of complaint, the willingness to keep on giving and keep on sharing, willing to sacrifice so that other children can have what they have. Your love really shines through them, and I am so honored, humbled, and blessed. May we all have children's hearts!

Well, as usual, we were in a hurry, but state agencies never are! By the time they had completed all the necessary paperwork and were ready, we were head long into a family crisis. Billy's daddy was diagnosed with cancer. Facing surgery, we delayed the girls' coming one week, but Billy said we could put it off no longer. We had been talking with the girls on the phone while they waited in a children's shelter in Texas. The girls knew they were coming to live with us. Billy did not want them to think that, yet again, they were not wanted or that they were being rejected.

So plane tickets were purchased for March 13th. The girls would be arriving at twelve noon with two adoption workers. Even with all the upset and turmoil surrounding my father-in-law's condition, we put the finishing touches on preparing for the girls' homecoming. I remember standing at their bedroom door going through my list of "moanies." Father, they don't have enough space for this or enough room for that, or enough closet space, etc... etc... etc. You just listened. After I finished moaning and was quiet, You agreed with me! You said, "You're right." To my utter amazement, You agreed with me! Then in Your still small voice You continued, "But they'll have a mama and daddy to love them and care for them, a Christian home and family, and someone to tell them all about Me." I was speechless. How can You say so much with so few words? So I quit my moaning, trusting that You know our needs and that You will keep Your promises of provision.

The big day arrived, with delays at every airport. The girls finally arrived at 6:00 p.m. Billy, myself, and Bethany, 7, (Oh, God, how that child had petitioned Heaven for a little sister to play with!) met them with balloons, stuffed animals, and love--hearts overflowing with love. We could finally hug our girls! Oh, God, You are so good! Thank You. Thank You for these precious miracles!

They were all so quiet, with smiles peeping out from behind their nervousness. We collected the luggage and were homeward bound where thirteen brothers and sisters were anxiously waiting. The kids had put balloons on the mailbox and all around the dining room with a "Welcome Home" banner included in the decorations. What a celebration! It's not every day that you get three new sisters, and they were determined to make the most of it!

Your words are truth. You said with Hebrews 6:14-15, "I will surely bless you and give you many descendants." And so after waiting patiently, (I am getting better at that part! Praise God!), I received what was promised! They were home! Our three new additions -- Charity Ruth Walker, Re-

Charity Ruth - So Precious!
11 years old

bekah Hope Walker, and little Lydia Faith Walker, ages seven, six, and five respectively, finally made it home.

Your workings never cease to amaze me; You are truly an awesome God! You brought three little girls into our lives and hearts the previous April, and here we were a year later with them at home were they belonged. I did hear You correctly. You meant for them to be here all along. It just had to be in Your timing. I thank You, Father, that Your word is true. What You promise, You will bring to pass, because You are the original Promise Keeper!

One month after their homecoming, I penned these words:

Tomorrow it will be one month--a month filled with prayer for emotional healing, a month with tons and tons of hugs and kisses, a month filled with "Which drawer is my underwear in?", a month filled with love and laughter, and yes, a few tears. Their tears at the overwhelming changes occurring so rapidly in their short lives and mine at the sadness of a child being five, six, or seven years old and not having someone in their life that they would cry or ask for. Then tears of blessedness that You chose us to be that someone for them. I remember the first "Mama", and the day they called Billy, "Daddy." We had eaten lunch and then walked down the hall to our room. Billy asked, "Did you hear what Rebekah said? What she called me?" I told him, no, I had not heard. He got this "proud Papa" look on his face and said, "She called me, Daddy!" Oh, Dear God, thank You for such a man as this that I can call my husband. You did good, God; You did real good!

So on the home front, things are settling down. Most of the time we can all remember whose clothes we moved to which closet a month ago. Ruth is hardly having bladder control problems anymore. Father, she is blossoming like a flower unfolding in Your "Son-shine"! Lydia is not having

Rebekah Hope's Science Project
8 years old

to get up two and three times every night to come give me a hug. Yeah, Father, I know. She just had to keep making sure I was here! And Rebekah . . . Rebekah has the answer to her all important question that she asked the first week they were home. After being here for several days, hearing us pray to Jesus, mention His name in Bible study and family devotionals, and hearing me say, "I gotta talk to Jesus", she looked up at one of her big sisters and asked her question, "Who is Jesus?"

People want to know how we do it. Oh Father, how could we not do it? So what, if the septic tank has to keep being pumped out because it wasn't meant to house this many people, and the washer and dryer runs from daylight to bedtime. I would run too if I were facing that mountain of clothes each day! What difference does it make that sixteen kids share four bedrooms and only two bathrooms, and that we cannot buy the large bulk supplies of groceries and gigantic pots that we need because we do not have cabinet nor storage space to put them? What does it matter that bath time starts at five o'clock and goes on until, or that someone usually winds up taking a cool bath? In the natural, these are minor inconveniences, but in the spiritual realm where You reign, of what Kingdom value are these sacrifices? What Kingdom value indeed? Three more little girls know the answer to the question -- "Who is Jesus?"

Your Abundantly Blessed Daughter,
Bonnie

Lydia Faith's Kindergarten Graduation
6 years old

Chapter Fourteen

An Open Garden . . .
To God Be the Glory

Dear Precious Father,

It's really funny how You blind us to the magnitude of things when we are in the middle of a situation. As the number of children increased, others around us were flipping out, but I couldn't figure out what the big deal was. We had seventeen at home with nine of those ranging from ages 9 years to 18 months. I honestly and truly couldn't see what all the hoopla was about. I didn't get the revelation until three or four years later. I was looking back at pictures one day taken during this time, and it just hit me. Oh, my goodness, we had a house full of babies. No wonder everybody was going nuts over what we were doing. As news spread by word of mouth about our unusual family adopting all these children, the media began to sit up and take notice. Your little girl had yet another cross to bear. One that felt awfully uncomfortable on her 'very private' shoulders.

It started in May of 2001 with a Mother's Day article on

the front page of the Macon Telegraph. Lord, You know that my prayer was that You would be glorified. I liked when Ed Grisamore wrote that we had filled our home with God's love and then filled it with children. I had prayed so hard that Your Holy Spirit would be the author of the article. You really shone through with the sentence about it being "too difficult to make temporary what Bonnie believed in her heart was meant to be permanent." That was anointed! It is the heartbeat that pulses through Your work here -- permanency -- loving unconditionally through the good and the bad. Thank You, Father, for allowing me to be a part of Your work. What a privilege!

Looking back, it was quite an experience. The kids had a blast. They thought is was so "cool" to be on the front page of the paper. How did You do that? You put an article about a family that loves You on the front page of a secular newspaper. You never cease to amaze me! Lord, I want to be used by You, but I need You to continually refresh me with a willing heart about this publicity stuff. With the 700 Club wanting to come do a story about us and all the other doors You were flinging open, Your little girl just wanted to run and hide. I prayed, "Strengthen me, Father, I need You!" I do not want to just be willing to be willing; I want to serve You in every area wholeheartedly, with a cheerful, willing heart. We had asked, like Jabez, that You "bless us indeed and enlarge our territory" (I Chronicles 4: 9-10). I saw these opportunities as an answer to that prayer, but my flesh screamed "No" at the thought of being in the public eye so much. I guess part of it was fear. No, come to think of it, most of it was fear! And yes, Lord, I know that fear is not from You.

You know that all the responses to the article were not positive. We took some pretty hard hits. I had sense enough to know that my dear Mama's words are so true, "The more you step out on the front lines for Jesus, the more you open yourself up for attacks." But You are worth it, and my heart does rejoice in Your promise of Matthew 5: 11- 12,

"Blessed are ye, when men shall revile you, and persecute you, and shall say all manner of evil against you falsely, for My sake. Rejoice, and be exceedingly glad; for great is your reward in heaven."

So thank You, Father, for using me. If one heart is touched and drawn nearer to You, it is worth it.

Then there was my fear of falling back into pride, trying to do the work by trusting in the arm of the flesh (II Chronicles 32:8), losing focus of You as my first priority (Colossians 1:18), and worshipping again the idol of busyness. Father, I do not want to sin against You. I don't want to hurt my sweet Jesus. I know the tendency of my sinful nature and the weakness of my flesh. You, Yourself, caution us to beware "let him that thinketh he standeth take heed lest he fall" (I Corinthians 10:12). I do not want to fall into sin nor fall out of fellowship with You, but I also know that I cannot sit on the bench when You have said 'play ball' either. So, I am trusting in Your grace to sustain me, "that thine hand might be with me, and that thou wouldest keep me from evil, that it may not grieve me" (I Chronicles 4:10). The Monday prior to Tuesday's interview, as we were trying to get ready, You convicted my heart about not worrying about the outside of the cup (what people see) but only be concerned with the inside (of our hearts -- where You see). As long as we allow You to keep the inside clean and pure, then people looking on the outside of our cups (our lives) will only see good -- the cleanness of Your Spirit. During our family Bible time the children received Your object lesson so well. You speak it so plainly, just like You did when You walked the earth. Even the little children can grasp Your meaning, so profoundly simple, so true, so wonderfully freeing! We prayed that You would cleanse our hearts and make us clean from the inside out. That we would not be overly concerned with temporal things, but that we would seek You and Your kingdom first and then "all these things [tasks that need to be accomplished] will be added unto [us]" (Matthew 6:33). Thank You for helping us keep the right focus, but You still had much work to do in me, as I was about to find out.

Hunting Buddies - Gabriel Samuel (4) & Adam Nathaniel (3)

I never knew when You led me to dub that summer 'Sacred Summer' what You fully meant, nor all You intended. Why do I keep thinking I understand what You are doing? Your thoughts and ways are certainly higher than mine (Isaiah 55:8-9). I thought that summer would be a nice time to just seek God a little more. How Your must chuckle at my ludicrous thought patterns! Late that Sunday night, when I called one of my prayer sisters for extra prayer coverage, I told her that I never dreamed during 'Sacred Summer' You would show me that I lived in 'Selfish City.' You revealed my selfish heart to me and the need for the Great Physician to carve out all the cancerous selfishness from my heart. Oh Father, how broken I was. I remember Billy asking me why was I so upset. My reply was because it is sin. It's ugly and it hurts my Jesus! Oh my sweet, sweet Jesus, I am so, so sorry! I remember through my tears looking up at my wonderful picture which I had recently purchased of Jesus laughing gloriously, and I knew this repentance was a good thing. You were so pleased that I had allowed You to spotlight the selfishness in my heart, asking You to cleanse me from it. I cried out for you to create in me a clean heart. As You well know a 'good thing' can sometimes be the hardest, most painful thing as well. Thank You for making me look into that mirror of Truth. "You shall know the Truth and the Truth shall set you free" (John 8:32). Thank You, Father, for freedom in You! Thank You! We humans have such a tendency to exalt ourselves in our thinking of "I'm not such a bad person. As a matter of fact, I'm doing pretty good for the Lord." Or at least this human does. Maybe Your other children do not struggle with that as much as I do, Father. You revealed to me that all those flare ups of anger and irritation were from selfishness because things were not going the way Bonnie wanted. Then You led me to look up the definition of selfishness, studying its every synonym in every dictionary we owned. My heart was broken! But broken hearts are a good thing when they are broken over sinfulness. You say in Psalms 34:18 that You are "near unto those who are of a broken heart." In Psalms 51:17, "The sacrifices of God are a broken spirit: a broken and contrite heart, O God, Thou wilt not despise." Just like You say in Isaiah 61, You came to "bind up the brokenhearted"; You certainly came to me that night, no condemnation, only love and joy. You were so happy Your little girl had finally realized the error of her ways. I guess I should say another one of the errors, shouldn't I , Father? Just as I was so blinded to this error, I am sure there are lots more hidden sins -- secret faults. It is so wonderful to know that even though for a time they may be hidden from me, they are never hidden from Your all seeing eyes, and Glory of Glory, You love me anyway! You are Wonderful, Wonderful! Oh God, I want to love like You love. I so want the mindset of Christ.

I couldn't stop crying the day You showed me that one of the most selfish things a person could do is be a 'closed garden.' Father, You told me with Song of Solomon 4:12, "A garden enclosed is my sister, my spouse, a spring shut up, a fountain sealed." I kept crying out to You "More, More!" Yet, I wasn't willing to sacrifice more of my time and energy so that more of You could shine and flow through me. That day in August, You finally got through to my hardened heart. I made a commitment to accept the responsibility that accompanied the more of You that I was so desperate for. When I did that, something in the spirit realm 'snapped.' There was a releasing of something You'd been wanting to send or do. I would no longer hold back the living water flowing through me, nor seal up the fountain of God's glory in my life. I embraced Your word to me in Song of Solomon 4:16, "Awake, O north wind; and come, thou south (Holy Spirit come) ; blow upon my garden (my spiritual growth process) that the spices (the fragrances of Your gifts, healing, and restoration) thereof may flow out (and bless others). Let my beloved (Jesus) come into His garden (of my life), and eat His pleasant fruits." May my sweet Jesus be pleased with the fruit He finds upon His vines!

Father, I had no idea of the magnitude of Your plans to which I was committing, but one thing I knew for sure. There was no going back and closing the gate. Even now the thought brings tears to my eyes. I liked my privacy and disdained the publicity, but strolling through my garden (my life) without You was an unimaginable horror that I could not even consider. I would obey You . For me, there was no other choice.

Your Committed Daughter,
Bonnie

Chapter Fifteen

Lights, Camera . . . And Holy Spirit!

Dearest Father,

It amazes me how You intricately weave the events of our lives together. David tells us in Psalms 139:16 that "All the days ordained for me were written in Your book before one of them came to be." What a gloriously comforting thought! So in July of 2000 when You said that You had prepared a 'divine appointment' for me, the events of that divine appointment were all ordained by You.

A friend had provided the money for me to attend a women's retreat in Mississippi. You told me ahead of time that You were going to use the divine appointment to provide for the work here at Refuge Ranch. So I was excited and expectant. I told the children to be praying because God was going to bless beyond anything we could possibly imagine. At the retreat, I knew instantly when Brooke Boland introduced herself as one of the writers and producers of the 700 Club that this was my divine appointment. That night she expressed her desire to do a story about us. I declined, telling her I did not like the idea of being on television. Lord, I had said I would be an open garden, but surely this wasn't what You meant! Well Brooke is kind of like You, she would not take no for an answer. You had already begun to endear to her heart the work here at Refuge Ranch, rescuing and restoring wounded children by placing them in permanent, loving, Christian families. That night You rebuked me for not utilizing Your blessing, Your provision. So, I went to Brooke the next morning. I told her that if she could figure out some way to do a story on us that would glorify You and not exploit our children (that was a large fear of mine) that I would talk about doing a show. We prayed about it together. I was supposedly "waiting on the Lord" as to timing and from what angle to approach this so that the children would not feel exposed and exploited. It must make You sick when we use that phrase, "waiting upon the Lord", after You have clearly told us to do something. Well, You know what happened next. I started back pedaling. I had drawn near to You with my lips, but my heart was far from You (Ezekiel 33:31) and Your plans for me. I had no intention of ever being on national television. I began to beseech You for "a ram caught in the thicket" (Genesis 22:13) as the provision, but I was a little more realistic than that. If I remember correctly the comments went something like this. "Okay, Lord, I have agreed to be on the 700 Club. Now You can start turning all those cow patties in the field into thousand dollar bills. I will pick them up, so we can use the money to add on to the house." Am I an idiot, or what? Do Your other children have such ridiculous conversations with You? Well anyway, You allowed my hesitance to rock on for six or seven months. Your patience amazes me. Then one day as I was crying out to You for provision for the house addition, You very calmly, very lovingly reminded me, "Bonnie, you have not used all of the resources I have provided." I knew immediately that You meant the 700 Club. I confessed and repented once again. I called Brooke the next morning. I laughingly told her that You had just finished spanking Your little girl, and I gave her permission to set up the shoot. I thought my prayer partners, who had been diligently beseeching heaven for our financial blessings, were going to "skin" me when they found out that I had been the hold up all this time. Bless their hearts. I deserved much more than their shocked expressions and their exclamations of "You mean you have been the hold up for the 700 Club not coming yet? You?"

Even when the 700 Club called in July to set the shoot up for August 17th, I declined once again because we had scheduled a home school cookout for that exact date. I still cannot believe my audacity at turning down an entire camera crew's scheduling plans. Talk about delayed obedience -- I get first prize in that department.

After several phone calls, I finally agreed to the 17th, because the producers thought the cookout would make good background footage. So here I am with all these home school families coming, and there You are chuckling because now everyone will have to be told in advance to expect a camera crew on the 17th. My plans had been to let the 700 crew quietly slip in and out without anyone being told. God, I assumed You had a really good reason for orchestrating it this way. Lord Jesus, I know You have been tempted in every way just like me, but You have never had to wake up to a camera in Your face. They wanted to spend all day with us -- cameras rolling. If I survived this adventure, I was going to tell everyone that You answer the Prayer of Jabez (even when Bonnie prays it). If Your children don't want their territory enlarged, they better remain silent. Again, my thoughts versus Your thoughts. I am thinking -- Yes, Lord, I'll care for more kids for You. You are thinking -- Oh great, she asked for 'more territory'; I'll put her on national television. Never, ever in my wildest dreams or even in my wildest nightmares would I have included national television. Lord, You do understand that I would not have done this for just anybody. Life with You is certainly interesting. I love You so much even though You won't let me play by 'my' plans. You are such a fun

God. I guess that is not an adjective that's attached to You much, is it? But here I am laughing with You over my own foolishness and silliness. So, I think You're fun. Thank You for loving me so much. To think that the God of all the universe wants to spend time with me, His child, and not just with me but with each one of His precious children is such an awesome thought, but then, You're an awesome God!

As August 17th dawned, I was getting up and facing one of the busiest days of my life, after having been up about three hours through the night with Joel. I nearly laughed with one of Terry Meeuwsen's first questions, "Do you ever sleep?" What a week we had already had. I remember when I finally got the revelation that You did not orchestrate the crew coming on the same day as the home school group just for Your glory, but it was also for our blessing. It amazes me how You can do one thing, and it folds right into Your plan to affect several facets of that plan at once. We would never have even survived that week had You not called on all our brothers and sisters to lend a hand. It was an entire week of blessings!

On Monday, You started out with free haircuts from a dear sister. Lord, I had not even realized how many of these children had never had a professional haircut. I usually just cut their hair myself because that is so much cheaper. But You provided beautiful hair cuts for free, and the children all felt like a million bucks. Thank You, Lord, for making them feel so special.

By Tuesday morning, I felt totally overwhelmed. With the help of volunteers, the new classroom addition was coming along, but we still had a ways to go. We finally had to hire carpenters for a few days to get us over the hump. Not only were we facing Friday's deadline with the camera crew, but school was to start on August 27th. We had already postponed it a week, and unless You performed a miracle, which You did, we were not going to make it. So with juggling carpenters, school preparation, and 700 Club preparation, I felt like a one-woman juggling act, and someone kept adding extra balls which were rapidly getting out of control. But You always meet us at our point of need. I wish the world knew how magnificently awesome You are. You began to touch hearts, and I am still overwhelmed at the response. Brothers and sisters began to volunteer left and right. Several churches offered to help with meals, to babysitting, yard work, and even painting the little girls fingernails. By this time all the kids had begun to feel like royalty, which they are, but as mama, I was getting a little concerned about all the attention spoiling them.

Joel Isaac - 5 years old

About 10:30 p.m. Thursday night, I remembered that I had not prepared part of the meal for Friday's dinner ahead of time like I had intended. We would be interviewing the next morning. For a few minutes I was tempted to stay up and get it ready. Thankfully, Your Holy Spirit won that round. Matthew 6:34 says, "Therefore do not worry about tomorrow, for tomorrow will worry about itself. Each day has enough trouble of its own." Hallelujah! It is a good thing I listened because at that moment Joel woke up. He had been sick all week with allergies, and he was also cutting teeth. It was late when I got him back to sleep. Poor baby, he was facing a really big day on a third of his normal sleep time.

Finally, everything that was going to get ready was ready. Each of the kids had three suits of clothes. One church blessed us so that each child had at least one "new" suit to wear. The children were so excited about the new clothes. Each suit was labeled for each child and numbered in order: suit 1, 2, and 3 with hair bows, accessories, and "new" matching socks that one dear, thoughtful lady had the foresight to bless us with. The house was cleaned, the yard was beautiful, the classroom was not finished, but had some semblance of order. All I wanted was that Your servants be found faithful. On Wednesday morning during my time with You, I "set my face like a flint" (Isaiah 50:7). I was determined I would finish this for You or die trying. You had allowed me to be secluded out here in my own little world, living in my own little garden. But now, You were saying that You wanted to bless others with the fragrance of Your wonderful love and mercy. Oh, Holy Spirit, blow! Sweet Jesus, You have torn down the fences surrounding my "enclosed" garden. You have brought me so far and set me free from so much bondage. More than I want my privacy, and more than I want the seclusion, Oh, Dear Jesus, I want people to know that Your word is true, that they really can have Your Abundant Life, "rivers of living water", flowing out of them (John 7:38). You remember years and years ago as I kept reading that verse, John 10:10. "I am come that [Bonnie] might have life, and that [she] might have it more abundantly." I knew even then that You could not lie. I remember telling You, "Well, Lord, You came so I could have an abundant life, and this ain't it. If this is as good as it gets, then You can just take me home." But that was not Your plan. You wanted to prove to Your somewhat rebellious little girl that Your Word is Truth. I had the head knowledge of that, but You wanted heart knowledge. Heart knowledge is the only knowledge that will create a change in lifestyles and actions. Boy, did my actions ever need changing!

Okay, back to Friday morning. Alex was supposed to meet the crew in Rhine at 8:30 a.m. The crew arrived on schedule: Terry Meeuwsen, the co-host, Cheryl Wilcox, the producer, along with two cameramen. Within ten minutes following the introductions, they began to rearrange our living room. As we chatted, the cameramen were extremely busy setting up lights, audio, and camera equipment. The boys were mesmerized with all the boxes of gadgets, cords, cameras, and lighting equipment. The girls were enchanted with Mrs. Terry, a former Miss America. With a couple of the kids tagging along as tour guides, Cheryl was busy casing the place inside and out, deciding what would make the best footage, the best shots, etc.

While the children could not get over their Daddy sitting still as Mrs. Terry put makeup on him, the crew could not get over Your peacefulness, Your calmness that reigns here. I was so honored to tell them it was Your Holy Spirit. He is the one whose presence they felt. Thank You for manifesting Your presence to them, Holy Spirit. I had prayed that they would feel You the minute that their feet touched the ground here at Refuge Ranch. You really showed up and showed out. Oh, Jesus, thank You for the precious gift of Your Spirit. Your Spirit had such control here that the producer even let the kids sit and listen to our interview which lasted about an a hour and a half. I cannot speak of Your blessings without crying. As I got to Joseph's story, he, too, began to cry. Father, I ask again that no emotional harm will come to these children who have so willingly agreed to have their stories told so that You might be glorified. That was a major hurdle of fear that I had to overcome in agreeing to do this in the first place. You are God enough to keep these kids from being exploited in any way. Guard them, sweet Jesus, guard them.

Next was lunch, consisting of baked ham, butterbeans, corn-on-the-cob, potato salad, a fruit bowl, macaroni and cheese, and homemade biscuits topped off with homemade peach jam. Within thirty to forty five minutes of finishing the interview, we sat down to eat. Terry kept asking how on earth I had done that. To tell the truth, I do not have a clue, so it could not have been me. I guess she did not see Your angel chefs flying around in our tiny kitchen. You are awesome! We went from eating, to changing clothes, to shooting classroom footage of Christy teaching the children while Terry and Cheryl washed and dried our dishes. Pamela (14) was so funny. She whispered to me, "Oh, it is so cool that someone 'famous' is washing our dishes." I walked over to Cheryl and

Terry telling them what she had said. They laughed. Then Terry in her calm, so down-to-earth way, walked over to Pamela and hugged her. She said "Honey, that didn't do a thing for those dishes." We all laughed again. Lord, there wasn't an uppity bone in her body. No wonder You have been able to use her so to glorify Yourself; You use the humble. Thank You for setting Christian examples like that before our children, Father. Pamela will never forget those words, nor the hug that accompanied them.

The kids' interviews were next on the list. Terry discussed with David (9) and Joseph (8) the baptism of their pet chicken the week before. She questioned the older ones about why they were thankful to be here. She finished with interviewing Katrina (17) and Christy (24) as biological children and asking them how they felt about having so many adopted siblings. Then it was clothes changing again for background footage of the kids in the pool. Cheryl, bless her heart, got in with them while those of us who were less brave watched from the sidelines. Our little Lydia (5) could not get in because of her cast. She had fallen from the trapeze bar on the swing set and broken her arm about three weeks earlier. So she blew bubbles at the rest of them from the side of the pool. Cheryl, the producer, took a special interest in a major beach ball game with Greyson. She taught six-year-old Rebekah how to blow air out her nose so she could put her head under water without water getting up her nose. We all clapped and cheered. I have noticed a marked boost in her self-confidence since then. You use the simplest things in the heart of a child to bring healing. Our time was running out, but they quickly got some footage of one of the boys helping their daddy feed cows. That is such a special thing with the boys, going to work with Daddy! Greyson (12), Ricky (10), David (9), Joseph (8), Gabriel (5), and Adam (4) will all wait at the wood fence in front of the house for hours, if necessary, to catch a ride with Daddy. Terry told Billy that he reminded her of a giant gym set with kids climbing all over him; that really tickled Billy. The rest of us were changing again, getting ready for our "Good-byes."

Oh, Father, what an experience. We had done our part; now the editing and the air time was in Your very capable hands. I felt like a balloon with the air slowly being released. We laid everyone, ages twelve and under, down for a nap and anyone else who felt the need! It was a much needed break because home school families would begin arriving in less than an hour.

Your Exhausted Little Girl,
Bonnie

Chapter Sixteen

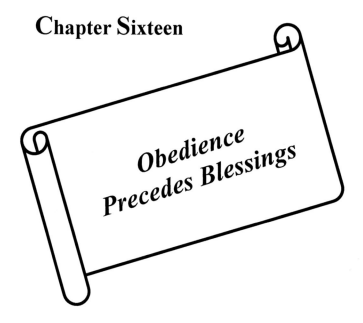

Obedience Precedes Blessings

Oh Father,

I really do not remember much I said or did the evening after the 700 Club left. During the home school cookout, I could answer a question if someone asked, but I could not carry on a running conversation. But Your grace is sufficient, and here again, You carried us. So many of the home school families blessed us by cooking and bringing food that night. A lot of them even went so far as to leave the extra food for us instead of carrying it home with them. Lord, for all the people we have accidentally forgot to thank through the years, whether their sacrifice was large or small, bless them double. We try to write down all the blessings, but honestly, at several points, they were pouring in so quickly we could not get them recorded fast enough. Let Your people know that You have not forgotten. In Your sovereignty, You saw and You remember. Remind them all how You blessed the widow's mite and the alms done in secret. Oh, Lord, of all the blessings, the prayers of Your saints are what enabled us to be victorious for You. I could literally feel the Pray-ers praying. I praise You for the Pray-ers, God! Bless them, bless them, bless them, in Jesus' name!

But our week of blessings continued. Earlier in the summer a youth group came to begin enlarging our classroom which we had outgrown. With four starting Kindergarten that year, we desperately needed more room. You again opened the windows of Heaven. The next morning another church family arrived with tools in hand to work on the classroom. Six of those precious men gave up their day of leisure to further Your ministry here at Refuge Ranch. I kept telling myself-- I am not going to cry; I am not going to cry! But I did! I told the workers I certainly could not pay them, and that I'd never be able to pray enough to "pray" them back for their kindness. For lunch, the church ladies came out with a feast, enough to feed an army. We feasted! By Saturday evening I felt that if one more person did something nice for me, I was going to bawl. After everyone was gone, I broke down. I cried over Your abundance of blessings. My heart was overwhelmed with awe and humility at being used by You. I cried for Your exceeding grace "above all I could ask or think" (Ephesians 3:20). I was exhausted, but my heart was full to overflowing. "My cup runneth over", and I am sipping from my saucer. I died a thousand deaths to get to this place, and Jesus, for every time I have died to self, and said "Yes" to You--You have exceeded my expectations a thousand fold. You say, "Bring all the tithes [my time, talents, money, my wants, my desires, my motives] into the storehouse [of God's Sovereign will], that there may be meat [spiritual food and training] in Mine house, and test Me now herewith, saith the Lord of hosts, if I will not open for you the windows of Heaven, and pour out for you a blessing [upon blessing, upon blessing], that there shall not be room enough to receive it." Truly once again You have proven the truth, the faithfulness, of Your Word! There truly was not room left in my heart to receive another blessing. To an Awesome God, a loving Father, who deserves all the Honor, Glory, and Praise, I bow my knee to YOU! You alone are God--my God! "As for me and my house, we will serve the Lord" (Joshua 24:15). And as little Gabriel (5) would say, "And all of God's people say -- Amen!"

Some of the excitement died down, and we settled into school and back to the normal routine. I guess technically, normal and the Walkers are not synonymous, but that's okay. What is normal? I'm not sure I even know. It is sort of funny, but I do not even think about being different until someone else points out that we are. I do not think about the backdoor slamming fifty million times a day (unless it wakes up Joel!). And no, I have never counted the number of times a day I hear the word "Mama". It is music to my ears. Hugs and kisses all day long are "normal." Brothers and sisters saying, "I am sorry; will you please forgive me?" is normal. Saying a prayer for the healing of a boo-boo, instead of kissing it, is normal. Father, to us all these things are our life -- or rather Your life in us. But I am glad to others we seem to be a "peculiar people" (I Peter 2:9). Just this week, You told me with Exodus 19:5-6, "if you will indeed obey My voice and keep My covenant, then you shall be a peculiar treasure to Me . . . you shall be to Me a kingdom of priests and a holy nation." Oh Father, I will gladly be peculiar for You, if that means You will treasure me—and treasure this family. You are certainly my Treasure—my "pearl of great price" (Matthew 13:46)! I adore You, my sweet Father. I adore You. "Bless the LORD, O my soul, and all that is within me, bless His holy name" (Psalm 103:1). And we do bless You, Lord!

Eighteen! Eighteen adoptions in twelve years. Nine of the eighteen within two years. Four of those in one month. Wow! That is totally awesome -- totally You! I stand in amazement at Your blessings.

As You know, we finalized on Ruth, Rebekah, and Lydia's adoption through Texas on October 1, 2001. Lord, we just did not feel Joseph could handle their adoption being finalized before his, since he had been here six months longer than they had. We were not concerned about him being jealous, but our concern was that he would be overcome with fear that we had changed our minds about adopting him. With everything he had been through (so many rejections), we did not want him suffering needlessly. Besides, the girls were doing great. They seemed totally unconcerned about "adoption dates," never questioning the finalization or the promised adoption party. So we decided to postpone telling them until Joseph's adoption was finalized at the end of the month on October 31st. Then we would have one huge adoption party for all four of them. I did not realize until the Tuesday night before Joseph's finalization on Wednesday, that our girls had not said anything -- dared not say anything, because it could remind us that we might not want to adopt them after all. Where with Joseph, he constantly reminded us lest we forgot. The girls dared not remind us lest we remembered and changed our minds. Oh Father, it just about broke my heart. I could not wait until the next morning to reassure them. "We are your forever family! You do not have to be afraid." Father, please give each child Your peace that passes all understanding (Philippians 4:7).

They were all so excited the next morning. We carried the twelve youngest children to the courthouse with us. We could not all fit in the judge's chambers. By this time, they had all decided that signing the papers to be adopted was pretty boring stuff. They just wanted to speed on home for the adoption party.

The older teens had decorated and prepared everything for the party. Hiding huge "adoption" stuffed animals all over the house to be located with riddles and clues is always a big portion of the fun. School had been canceled for the day. There was no way to get fifteen kids who were that excited to sit down and concentrate, so I took pity on our two poor teachers. Besides the children had had an extremely educational field trip to the courthouse. They could make up the classwork another day. Oh, the beauty and flexibility of home schooling. Thank You, Jesus. It adds to our family time and togetherness so much. Thank You. We topped our day off with a family trip to the cow sale with Billy. Several had never been before, so they were excited.

Ruth (7) summed it up for all of us. She walked over to me and gave me a great big hug. Looking up at me with that wonderfully, peaceful smile, she said, "Mama, this has been a good day!" Oh Jesus, it brings tears to my eyes even now. How wonderfully precious are Your children! How dear -- how loving! Father, I have told You before, but it bears repeating. I do not know why You chose me to be the recipient of such blessings, but I am so glad You did. So Glad!

Adoption Party!
Rebekah (6), Ruth (7), Lydia (5) & Joseph (8)

I also want to thank You for a special memory. A few days after Joseph's adoption, we received Joseph's certified copy of the adoption order in the mail. You remember as I was reading to him the part about how he was permanently Joseph

Chuck Walker, son of Billy & Bonnie Walker. The little fellow, with a grin on his face and a twinkle in those sky blue eyes, asked, "Will it come off?" Puzzled, I questioned, "Will what come off?" He mischievously quipped back, "You said it was permanent -- like permanent marker. So I just wondered would it come off?" Oh Father, the joy of permanency! I belong! This is my home! Father, if I have not thanked You lately for adopting me -- Thank You! Like Joseph, I'm so glad that You did it with a permanent marker. I love You, Lord!

Your Adopted Daughter,
Bonnie

Chapter Seventeen

Television Debut

Well Abba,

You did it! April 24, 2002, will be a day these children re-member for the rest of their lives --- their television "debut" on the 700 Club. They thought it was so neat to be on national television. Even three days before the shoot aired, they were bouncing off the walls. The day before the actual showing, when the promotional ads came on, you could not even hear the television for kids exclaiming, "Look, there's me!" It amazes me when I think from where some of these kids have come from (some did not even have a home, much less a tele-vision set) and here You have put their smiling faces on an internationally watched television program. I am over-whelmed at the lengths to which You will go to make Your children feel special. Thank You, Father, for loving us so very much. You are not content to just save us. You want us to know, to really know, that Your hand and Your heart is near to "the least of these" (Matthew 25:40). You love us beyond our wildest imaginations, and You will do whatever it takes to prove it. For these children, some of whom came here with all their earthly belongings in one grocery bag, it was a really big deal. It made them feel valuable and important. Father, only You know how desperately needed that still is in some of their lives. Most of their self-esteems have been ripped to shreds and trampled on by the enemy. I praise You that You are in the restoration business. Deliverance and restoration is what You are all about. And love -- more love than I can even begin to imagine.

For me, it was a day of fighting back tears. Father, I have been obedient to You about Refuge Ranch just because You said so. That was all the reason I needed. You said do this, so I have. But once the e-mails and phone calls started pouring in from families (mostly foster and adoptive) all across the country, and even some emails from other countries, I was totally overwhelmed with the "needs" of Your people. Many were needing advice, help, and training. Many were encouraged to see what You can do in a home where Your Spirit is Lord. One lady said that she had invited the Holy Spirit into her home after watching the show. That really made me cry, because I knew it pleased You so much! Another dear sister emailed that they were encouraged to continue to fight the true enemy, Satan, for custody of four little girls in their home. I love her realization saying, "We are not fighting for physical custody, but for eternal custody of these children's souls!" Father, that is profound! I wish every Christian parent would get that revelation. Some of Your people were wanting tips on keeping Your peace continually abiding in their homes, while others just wanted to encourage us to keep up Your good work. Some wanted advice about individual situations with their own adopted children; then there were others who were "inspired" to adopt. I have wondered several times since the show just how many children You have placed in adoptive homes because You used our story to show people what You can do in restoring these children's lives. So I have cried and cried some more.

I received a major revelation through this. You used the

700 Club shoot to reveal to me the "need" for Refuge Ranch. These adoptive families need the Christian support from others who understand where they are coming from and what they are dealing with. One thing that echoed through nearly every email was, "It is such an encouragement to know someone else who has the same heart to adopt. We don't get any support at all in the area where we live." Father, with this overwhelming outcry for help, I can only reply, "Here am I! Send me." (Isaiah 6:8).

The previous fall You had kept telling me that it was 'the fullness of time'! You said that You were fixing to call, and I was to obey immediately. Not to offer any excuses, just obey. You even asked me if I was ready to be part of a miracle. You said with Acts 26:16, "rise and stand on your feet; for I have appeared to you for this purpose, to make you a minister and a witness both of the things which you have seen and of all the things which I will yet reveal to you." With II Chronicles 16:9, You said that You were looking for someone to show Yourself strong through. My heart's response was, "Lord, whatever You ask, my answer is yes!"

Near the end of the year, You sent a heavenly visitor. I was sitting in our bedroom holding Joel when I realized we were not alone. An angel stood in the room. The angel was huge, taller than our bedroom door, but he didn't have to lower his head to step into the room. The angel had a message for me. I didn't hear him with my natural ears, but with my spirit. His message was short and to the point, "Now is the time!" And here I was five months later answering Your call.

So many hurting, hungry souls were crying out. They needed to know of Your love and restoration power. I remember as a child the game we would play with a flower, pulling each petal off reciting, "He loves me, he loves me not." I praise You, Lord, that Your love is not like that. It is constant, all consuming, never-ending! Thank You. Thank You for teaching me of Your love. I had been pondering how most of Your children do not accept Your unconditional love. So many times, we feel the urge to perform to earn Your love. If we stumble today, the enemy tells us that we must do penance and feel guilty and down trodden for a sufficient length of time before we are "worthy" enough to come into Your presence again. Oh Father, I was in bondage to that for so long. How the enemy has duped and lied to Your children. Father, I ask, in Jesus' name, that You pour out Your truth on Your children, Your church as a whole. You loved us before we ever loved You. Your word tells us in II Corinthians 5:21 that You took our sin so "that we might become the righteousness of God in Christ." Thank You, Lord, that You provided a way for me to have continual access to You, even and especially when I have messed up. You know that when our children here at home sin and mess up we do not say, "Well, you messed up today, and we are not going to love you until you have been miserable long enough." We do not withhold hugs and kisses until they have learned their lesson. How much more loving is our heavenly Father to His children! Nothing hurts a parent's heart like a child rejecting that parent, not coming to the parent when the child has a need. So, if we do not come to You when we are sin-sick, that must really hurt You.

Forgive us Father, in Jesus' name. Open our eyes and show us Your love. For years there was a secret longing deep within me, "Love me, please love me unconditionally." Even though You did love me, for years I could not feel that love because I was so blinded by the enemy's lies. "You messed up again. You keep sinning the same sin over and over. You are not really sorry. God hates sin, so you are not *good* enough to really be His child." Then those feelings of disconnection would engulf me along with discouragement, depression, and hopelessness. "Well, I tried my best and I just cannot make it. I can't keep from falling back into sin." Oh Father, it is all so easy, but I was so deceived that I could not see. It was not my "sinless" state that made You love me in the first place. You loved me before I ever knew You. Romans 5:8 says, "But God demonstrates His own love toward us, in that while we were still sinners, Christ died for us." While I was still a sinner, lost, rejecting You, You died for me. Oh Praise You, Jesus. I had heard that all my life, but in my heart I did not believe it. I did not feel it. Oh Father, what misery! All my life I had felt driven to "perform" for acceptance. The performing had become such a burden. You say in Your word that, "My yoke is easy and My burden is light" (Matthew 11:30). Well, what I was carrying and doing was not easy nor light. It is so funny what I found in an old journal the other day. I had written the following words,

"Oh God, I can't tend to any more children. I can't even care for the six we have now."

Camouflage Boys - March 2001
Adam (5), Gabriel (5), Joseph (8), Greyson (12),
Joel (18 months), Ricky (11), & David (9)

So overwhelmed, so burdened, so in bondage! Here I am years later with nearly four times that many children and all I can say is, "You are awesome!" Trying to care for six children in my own strength, trusting in "the arm of the flesh" (Jeremiah 17:5), my own abilities and capabilities, depending on "me", I was failing. But when You, the "new creature" within me, has control, You truly become the "I" in "I can do all things" (Philippians 4:13). I did not understand that truth nearly sixteen years ago when You called us to this ministry, but I understand now. I rejoice, oh Father, how I rejoice. I can be Your little girl, dancing around Your feet, rejoicing in Your presence, Your Love. I do not have to do a thing, just be with You, basking in Your adoration, Your love, and Your acceptance. Oh dear, sweet, precious Father, I praise You that I do not have to be "distracted with much serving" (Luke 10:41). I thank You, Father, that "one thing is needed" and You rejoice with me that I have "chosen that good part, which will not be taken away" (Luke 10:41-42) from me. I have wanted a daddy like You all my life. I had tried to get Your love and acceptance from my earthly Daddy, and then I even placed that yoke on Billy for years. But the truth is -- it does not matter how loving and attentive any human is, they can never consistently love like You love! Nobody else could fill that longing of my heart to be loved, to be accepted just like I am. Good days, bad days -- good ways, bad ways! Oh Father, how gloriously wonderful to be adopted by You! Thank You so very much. Now I am free to serve You and let Your Spirit and Your power flow through me. I am not bound by "have to's" and "I must's". I am free to serve You out of a heart of love, out of a "want to" heart, not a "have to" heart. Father, it is so much fun! You have proven once again that Your Word is truth. For Your yoke truly is easy, and Your burden truly is light (Matthew 11:30). You are a never-ending source of delight. Lord, help me show Your unconditional love to these little ones here and to each and every person that You bring into my life!

"The Holy Spirit said,

'Now separate to Me. . . for the work to which I called them" (Acts 13:2).

Father, You spoke this to my heart so clearly that there was no misunderstanding. Now was the time to start sharing with others what You in Your grace and mercy shared with me. "Behold the hand servant of the Lord! Let it be to me according to Your word" (Luke 1:38).

Your Humbled Daughter,
Bonnie

Chapter Eighteen

God's Amazing Ways . . .
Pregnant Again!

My Dear Father,

You are so marvelous in all Your ways. As You placed us more and more in the public eye, speaking invitations increased accordingly. Women's retreats, churches, adoption banquets, and Mother's Day celebrations all were opportunities to proclaim Your amazing works and ways. As the fame of Your work here was broadcast, You touched more and more hearts wanting to pour into the ministry of blessing these children. One dear group of brothers came and closed in the carport which blessed us with another bedroom. Praise You, Lord. I had said that we had five bedrooms for so long that it almost seemed strange to say six bedrooms. The middle boys were so excited with their new room. Psalms 118:23 says, "the Lord has done this, and it is marvelous in our eyes."

You performed other marvelous works as well. During the summer of 2003, a dear church family donated a modular classroom leaving us in complete awe of Your amazing ways. It was a very busy summer. Our brothers (I call them Your carpenters!) kept showing up time after time. Thanks to You and their tireless efforts, Your new classroom was finished. You put in six closets, a brand new roof, turned one of the half baths into a complete bathroom, installed beautiful new underpinning, hooked up the air conditioning at a fraction of the original cost, replaced the ceiling, moved cabinets from the old classroom, and covered the entire trailer floor with new carpet. I was tearfully and wonderfully amazed. Maybe I should not be, but I was. You did not wave a magic wand and touch the trailer to achieve this transformation; You touched hearts -- heart after heart, after heart! So many of our precious brothers and sisters have given, helped, and shared! We had never experienced such a season of Your favor through Your children who just wanted to help. It is so astounding and humbling. There have been so many free Saturdays forfeited to come and work in the intense summer heat, so many love offerings and donations, so many tirelessly praying, and so many left at home who cheerfully sacrificed time with husbands, daddies, and grandpas just so the men in their families could come and do the work here. Giving, giving, giving! Oh Father, how wonderful! They were all copying You! Where is that verse about being imitators of You as dear children? Oh yes, Ephesians 5:1-2. Verse two tells how we are supposed to imitate You -- by walking in love. Well, Father, You have a lot of children surrounding us who do exactly that. Walk in love! And just as You received Christ's offering and sacrifice as a sweet-smelling aroma (Ephesians 5:2) that reached clear to Heaven, may each of these precious saints' offerings and sacrifices be a sweet-smelling fragrance to You as well. May rich blessings be poured out on each one, Lord. I ask this in Jesus' sweet and precious name.

I pray You were pleased with Your classroom's dedication service. I felt that since it is Your trailer, Your words should be written on it. The children had so much fun writing Bible verses on the floor. Of course, this was before we got our beautiful new carpet. Father, I still could barely believe it. We had just resigned ourselves to accept that we would just have to paint the floor and make do. But You are not in the "just making do" business! You touched a brother's heart, and he not only donated the carpet, but the labor as well. But back to the dedication ceremony, as each child read their Bible verse and thanked You, my eyes brimmed with tears. I confessed to the children how I had looked and looked for a trailer or an old house in which to have school.

Looking back, some of the ones I had considered were nothing but dumps that I was willing to "settle" for, but You were not! You had told me that previous fall that You had something better. Oh, how gloriously true to Your word that You are! Thank You, Lord. Your better certainly proved best. Even after all of Your provision, You would think that I would have learned. Through our brothers and sisters in Christ, You paid for a new roof and new skirting for the trailer. When a tree uprooted during heavy rains and fell across the trailer ruining part of the new roof, once again I thought we would have to patch and make do. But once again, You touched a heart and the dear brother donated roofing and labor to repair it. You are an awesome God! This brother had grown up in a children's home and the difference in the life he had and the one that You have provided here for these kids brought tears to his eyes. Bless him, Father, for caring for "the least of these" (Matthew 25:40).

Toward the end of August, Joel (3) had had about all he could handle of his mama focusing on getting the new class-room set up. I had been painting for about a month. I had re-painted all the kids' desks. We had only spray painted them the first time several years ago. So this time, we got a little more creative. I painted anything on them from a tiger to a dirt bike, from a John Deere emblem to a giraffe or a coon dog. Whatever struck each child's fancy became the theme for his or her desk. After finishing up with the desks, I had started doing some painting in the classroom. This was where Joel decided enough is enough. Very calmly, very wistfully, one day he stated, "Mama, I'm tired of you painting." He wanted his mama back! Oops! I did it again. I had become so involved in the natural stuff that needed doing that I had lost focus of the "most important" things that needed doing.

It is amazing how Your voice sounds so much like the voice of my children sometimes. I definitely needed reminding of how subtly my focus had shifted. You are always more interested in our relationships with those around us than in tasks to be accomplished, and I should be, too. Joel's plea did not come from a spoiled child demanding attention, but from the yearning heart of a child longing for more time with his mama. How quickly we neglect the most important things for the temporal, earthly things. Needless to say, I retired my paintbrush. Still more painting to be done? Yes. But it was not urgently demanding completion, or if it was, I could no longer hear it screaming for my attention because my focus was drawn back to a small child who needed me more. Father, show me the balance. I am such an extremist, throwing myself so whole-heartedly into every task. It is all or nothing with me. By the way, You still have not explained to me why I am that way. I know, I know! All in Your timing! My asking so many questions has sure got me into a lot of trouble, but I have also learned a lot. So, Holy Spirit, please teach me "balance." Jesus said You would teach me all things (John 14:26), and I desperately need training in that area. One of the things I have learned is that You delight in lavishing gifts on Your children. These past few years were filled with gifts straight from the throne room of Heaven. From two washers and dryers installed free to vacations at beach houses loaned out to us by friends, You continually poured out Your blessings.

Another thing that I've learned is that the only thing constant, besides You and Your love, is change. Change, change, change! One day I was lamenting the fact of constant change. As the children grow up, move out, and get married it is almost always what I call fruit basket turnover. And Father, fruit basket turnover is exhausting! On this particular occasion, I so wanted my "nest" built. I wanted completion and everything set up and organized. You brought me up short

Blessed Christmas, 2003
1st Row: Adam, Ruth, Lydia, Josey, Joel, Katrina, Anna
Bethany, Rebekah & Gabriel
2nd Row: Ricky, Alex, Pamela, David, Greyson, Diana,
Weston & Joseph

with Philippians 2:14. "Do all things without complaining", Ouch! There I was complaining, even if it was only in my heart, about the constant, on-going juggling, moving, and re-arranging. The very things You were sending to bless me, I was allowing to bring unrest into my soul. Thank You, Father, for Your forgiveness of my foolish, childish whining. I repented of my ways. My prayer now is: "May there always be change and growth on Refuge Ranch. May there always be construction, additions, and multiplications. And may we always, always see these things as blessings from our Father's loving hands and not begrudge the temporary inconvenience to our flesh." You are so wonderful and so very loving.

I remember well Your love shining through in a powerful way in January of 2005. Billy really hadn't felt well for quite some time, but as You know he was sick most of December with one illness after another. It was a nightmare when we had to call the ambulance to pick him up. He'd been sick again with sinus and chest congestion. His temp was 103, and he had started having hard chills. Once the chills started, things quickly spiraled down hill from there. By the time he turned gray and nauseous, I was afraid that he was having a heart attack. It was quite an unnerving event. All the older children had arrived by the time the ambulance got here. Later, they told me that I had scared them worse than their Daddy being sick. I usually have some kind of idea about nursing someone when sickness strikes, but Billy was manifesting so many varying symptoms that I was clueless. I did all I knew to do, sponge him with cool rags and PRAY! At one point Billy became delirious and was mumbling something about picking apples. Now the kids tease him about going to pick apples, but at the time it was not funny one bit. At the hospital, they diagnosed Billy with a severe kidney infection and diabetes. He had already been loosing weight because he had been so sick, but by the time we came home he had lost a total of 30 pounds. I praise You, Father, for keeping him safe.

Katrina was so upset about having to go back to college with her Daddy still in the hospital. As I walked her out of the hospital, I reassured her that this was Your provision to restore her Daddy's health. You have truly done just that. He felt better than he had in five years. I had forgotten how much he loves teasing and poking fun at people -- me in particular! He laughed one day and remarked, "You don't know what to do with me now that I feel good." Oh Father, thank You for returning my husband to me and giving these children their daddy back to them. We praise You, Lord.

By the time April rolled around, You had healed and restored his health so that Billy was not even having to take any diabetic medication. He had totally eliminated sugar from his diet, and his sugar was remaining perfectly normal. But the incident had shook us both more than either of us realized. We still had 14 children at home to raise. So by summer we very gradually came to a mutual decision. We retired! We quit! We were finished! Or so we thought! We wouldn't say one hundred percent, but when people asked were we through adopting we would say something like this: "Well, we think so. Twenty-one is a good number. It's seven (the number of completion) three times over. We've probably done our share." The only thing that kept me from writing it in cement was some scriptures that You'd given me several times over the past few years about more children coming. But following my fear instead of Your Spirit, I tried to justify it away. I am so glad that when You want to get Your children's attention, You say it clearly and loudly. You even confirm Your "word by the signs that accompanied it" (Mark 16:20b).

In our retirement plans, we made one major mistake. We forgot to ask You what You had to say about it. I should be wise enough to know better, but oh well! . . . At the end of August, we received a phone call about a birth mom looking for an adoptive family for her twins. I had always wanted twins, but due to our recent decision I didn't get all excited about the call. Later that day, I shared the phone conversation with Billy and got the shock of my life. I told him the situation, and the first words out his mouth went like this. "Well, we just need to make sure that the birth mom has insurance of some kind, because we can't afford a big hospital bill." Father, a bolt of fear shot through me as I gripped the arms of the recliner so hard my knuckles turned white. Billy continued to talk along those lines until finally I overcame the shock, regained my voice, threw up my hands and said, "Wait, wait, wait! I didn't say I wanted them." His reply to that was, "Huh? Well make up your mind. I wouldn't mind having another little one in the house." Father, what planet did You get this man of mine off of? He collects kids like most men collect junk for their favorite hobby. I was terrified. At least I knew what to do with the fear. I fell on my face before You! "I had to know what You had to say about all this. I was already forty-seven, and Billy would join me in just a few days. We had to know what our Father wanted us to do.

In the height of my fear, I exclaimed to Billy, "We don't

have room for twins, nor the money, nor the time, or energy." But the big thing was not enough space! I called a prayer partner asking her to pray. Unbeknown to me, that night she asked You to give us a very clear sign. How You must have chuckled!

The next morning about 9:30 a.m., a lady called saying that her husband wanted to come over that morning to see about adding on to our house. Sure enough he showed up about eleven o'clock and wanted to head up a team of businessmen willing to add approximately 2,000 square feet on to our existing 2,400 square foot home -- at no cost to us.

Father, I would have had to be spiritually daft not to have connected the two incidents together -- the phone call about twin babies and the men wanting to enlarge the house. It wasn't until I called my prayer partner that evening that I realized exactly what You had done. I called to share the exciting news about the house, and her reaction was laughter. She started chuckling and couldn't stop. I asked, "What is it? What is so funny?" She finally managed to say to me, "Well, I asked God to give you a very clear sign about getting the twins!" We needed more space for more kids! Father, I heard You loud and clear!

That particular set of twins didn't work out, but You had our attention once again. We updated our home study and watched in awe as You nearly doubled the size of our home. You are so amazing! I found a scripture that You had given me on August 16, 1994. With Deuteronomy 6:10-11, twelve years earlier, You had promised me a house that I did not build. Once again my God, my dear Abba, You kept Your word.

With You changing the desires of our hearts, I felt pregnant again. This time it was Joel (6) who was being clingy. How much longer would it be Lord? From what direction or source would they come? How many were coming this time? I was full of questions and full of expectancy. I had been here before. For months You had kept saying with Luke 1:35,

"The Holy Spirit will come upon you, and the power of the Highest will overshadow you. . .".

19th Anniversary - Renewal of Wedding Vows
Billy teasing Bonnie about a 2nd Honeymoon

There I sat again in Your spiritual delivery room . . . waiting for the birthing of yet another miracle. My response? "Yes, Lord! Be it unto me according to Thy Word!"

My one desire with my every heartbeat was that You be glorified more than ever before . . . nothing else really mattered. Not our age, or Billy's health! Nothing! Nothing except being obedient to You! I love You so much Abba -- so much!

Your Pregnant Daughter,
Bonnie

If you would like more information about Refuge Ranch and our Ministry,
You may contact us at:

www.refugeranch.com

74 Billy Walker Road
Rhine, GA 31077

email address: hinds_feet@hotmail.com

*If you'd like more information on adoptions
or helping orphans,
please feel free to contact one of the
following agencies:*

<u>Covenant Care Services</u>
1-800-226-5683

**3950 Ridge Avenue
Macon, GA 31210**

<u>*www.covenantcareadoptions.com*</u>

✟

<u>*Christian Alliance for Orphans*</u>

<u>*www.christianalliancefororphans.org*</u>

Email:
info@christianalliancefororphans.org

✟

<u>*Orphan's Promise*</u>
1-800-730-2537

**977 Centerville Turnpike
Virginia Beach, VA 23463**

<u>*www.orphanspromise.org*</u>

2146337

Made in the USA